Unleashing Your Inner Potential: The Power of Mindset Mastery

by Madison Henderson

Unleashing Your Inner Potential: The Power of Mindset Mastery
Madison Henderson
Copyright ©2023 Madison Henderson. All Rights Reserved.
ISBN: 9781778900273
Imprint: Matti Charlton

This self-help book is a transformative guide that empowers you to unlock your true potential and achieve lasting success. With a focus on mindset mastery, this book reveals the untapped power of your mind and teaches you how to harness it to overcome obstacles and achieve remarkable growth.

From understanding the mind-body connection to cultivating a growth mindset, embracing challenges, and utilizing the art of visualization and affirmations, you'll learn to break free from limiting beliefs and self-sabotaging patterns. Navigate your thoughts and emotions with emotional intelligence, gratitude, and positivity. Build resilience, set purposeful goals, and overcome procrastination to take meaningful action.

Nurturing relationships, empathy, effective communication, healthy boundaries, and mentorship play crucial roles in your personal growth journey.

Sustain your progress through self-care, mindfulness practices, self-compassion, and a lifelong learning mindset.

Reflect on your journey, embrace your transformed self, and witness the remarkable results.

This book is a comprehensive roadmap to unleash your inner potential and live a life of fulfillment, abundance, and happiness.

Discover the power of mindset mastery today and embark on a transformative journey towards achieving your wildest dreams.

Unleashing Your Inner Potential: The Power of Mindset Mastery

by Madison Henderson

Table of Contents

I. Introduction 11
The Power of Mindset: Setting the Stage for Personal Growth
- The Power Within: Understanding the Influence of Mindset
- Unearthing Limiting Beliefs: Breaking Free from Self-Imposed Constraints
- Breaking the Chains of Self-Sabotage: Embracing Your True Worth
- The Power of Possibility: Transforming Challenges into Opportunities
- Cultivating a Resilient Mindset: Bouncing Back from Setbacks

Understanding the Mind-Body Connection
- The Mind-Body Connection: A Holistic Perspective
- The Power of Thoughts: Shaping Your Reality

II. Unleashing Your Inner Potential 37
Identifying Limiting Beliefs and Self-Sabotaging Patterns
- The Power of Beliefs: Unveiling Your Inner Landscape
- Unmasking Self-Sabotaging Patterns: Breaking Free from the Cycle
- The Empowering Shift: Cultivating a Growth Mindset

Cultivating a Growth Mindset: Embracing Challenges and Failures
- Embracing Challenges: A Gateway to Growth
- Learning from Failures: Building Resilience and Gaining Wisdom

The Art of Visualization and Affirmations
- Visualization: Painting Your Path to Success
- Affirmations: Empowering Your Inner Dialogue

III. Mastering Your Thoughts and Emotions 79
Taming the Inner Critic: Overcoming Negative Self-Talk
- The Nature of the Inner Critic
- Recognizing Your Inner Critic
- Challenging and Overcoming the Inner Critic

Emotional Intelligence: Navigating and Harnessing Emotions
- Understanding Emotional Intelligence
- The Importance of Emotional Intelligence
- Developing Emotional Intelligence

The Power of Gratitude and Positivity
- Understanding Gratitude
- The Power of Gratitude
- Practicing Gratitude
- Fostering Positivity
- The Power of Positivity
- Practicing Positivity

IV. Building Resilience and Taking Action 123
Developing Resilience: Bouncing Back from Setbacks
Understanding Resilience
The Elements of Resilience
Strategies to Develop Resilience
Navigating Setbacks and Building Resilience
Setting Purposeful Goals and Creating an Action Plan
The Power of Purposeful Goals
Creating an Action Plan
Overcoming Procrastination and Building Healthy Habits
Overcoming Procrastination and Creating Healthy Habits
Understanding Procrastination
Creating Healthy Habits

V. Nurturing Relationships and Support Systems 167
Cultivating Empathy and Effective Communication
Understanding Empathy
Effective Communication
Building Healthy Boundaries and Relationships
Understanding Boundaries
Building Positive Relationships
The Role of Mentorship and Accountability
Understanding Mentorship
Accountability for Personal Growth

VI. Sustaining Personal Growth 211
Self-Care and Mindfulness Practices
Understanding Self-Care
The Power of Mindfulness
Incorporating Self-Care and Mindfulness into Your Life
Celebrating Progress and Practicing Self-Compassion
The Power of Celebrating Progress
Practicing Self-Compassion
Incorporating Celebration and Self-Compassion into Your Journey
Embracing a Lifelong Learning Mindset
The Power of Lifelong Learning
Strategies for Embracing Lifelong Learning

VII. Conclusion 255
Reflecting on Your Journey and Embracing Your Transformed Self
The Power of Reflection
Celebrating Your Accomplishments
Embracing Your Transformed Self
Conclusion

I. Introduction

The Power of Mindset: Setting the Stage for Personal Growth

Welcome to a transformative journey of self-discovery and empowerment. In this section, we will embark on a profound exploration of the power of mindset and its remarkable influence on personal growth. Prepare to dive deep into the inner workings of your mind, unlocking the hidden potential that lies within.

The Power Within: Understanding the Influence of Mindset

Your mindset is not merely a fleeting state of mind; it is the foundation upon which your entire life is built. It shapes your beliefs, attitudes, and perceptions, ultimately determining the choices you make and the actions you take. Consider it the lens through which you view the world—a lens that can either limit your potential or expand it exponentially. By understanding the power of mindset, you hold the key to unlocking a future brimming with success, fulfillment, and joy.

At the core of personal growth lies a mindset that has the power to propel you forward: the growth mindset. Coined by renowned psychologist Carol Dweck, the growth mindset is a transformative perspective that sees challenges as opportunities, failures as stepping stones, and setbacks as mere detours on the path to success. Unlike its counterpart, the fixed mindset, which believes that abilities and intelligence are fixed traits, the growth mindset embraces the belief that your potential can be developed through dedication, effort, and a willingness to learn. By adopting the growth mindset, you open yourself up to a world of unlimited possibilities.

Unearthing Limiting Beliefs: Breaking Free from Self-Imposed Constraints

Within the depths of your subconscious mind, there may reside beliefs that silently hold you back from reaching your full potential. These limiting beliefs act as invisible barriers, constraining your growth and stifling your dreams. It's time to unearth them, examine their validity, and replace them with empowering beliefs that align with the extraordinary person you are becoming. This process requires deep introspection, self-awareness, and a willingness to challenge your long-held assumptions. Prepare to embark on a journey of self-discovery as you identify and release these self-imposed constraints, allowing your true potential to flourish.

Breaking the Chains of Self-Sabotage: Embracing Your True Worth

Self-sabotage can be a silent saboteur, hindering your progress and preventing you from realizing your true worth. It often stems from deep-rooted fears, insecurities, or a lack of self-belief. To break free from the chains of self-sabotage, you must first cultivate self-awareness and self-compassion. Explore the patterns and behaviors that hold you back, examine their underlying causes, and learn to embrace your true worth. This journey requires courage, vulnerability, and a willingness to confront the shadows within. As you release self-sabotaging patterns and embrace your authentic power, you will witness a remarkable transformation unfold.

The Power of Possibility: Transforming Challenges into Opportunities

In the realm of personal growth, challenges are not roadblocks but gateways to transformation. They provide us with opportunities to learn, evolve, and discover our hidden strengths. By shifting your perspective and reframing challenges as opportunities for growth, you can harness their transformative potential. Instead of shrinking in the face of adversity, you will rise, armed with resilience and a deep belief in your ability to overcome. Embrace the discomfort, face adversity head-on, and emerge stronger, wiser, and more resilient than ever before. Your journey toward personal growth begins by accepting the power of possibility in every challenge you encounter.

Cultivating a Resilient Mindset: Bouncing Back from Setbacks

Resilience is the armor that shields you from the blows

of life and propels you forward in the face of adversity. By developing a resilient mindset, you can bounce back from setbacks, navigate uncertainty, and emerge triumphant. Resilience is not a fixed trait; it is a skill that can be cultivated through intentional practice and a shift in mindset. It involves adapting to change, reframing failure as feedback, and cultivating a sense of inner strength. Through proven techniques and strategies, you will cultivate the mental fortitude to weather life's storms, learn from setbacks, and continue your journey toward personal growth with unwavering determination.

Embrace the power within your mind. With each word, idea, and revelation, you are stepping closer to unlocking your true potential. As we continue to explore the power of mindset, remember that your beliefs shape your reality, and your thoughts pave the way for personal growth. Prepare to transcend limitations, rewrite your story, and embrace the transformative power of a mindset aligned with your highest aspirations. The journey has just begun, and the possibilities are infinite.

Quiz Questions for Section I.A: The Power of Mindset: Setting the Stage for Personal Growth

1. What is the main focus of Section I.A?
2. **True or False**: Your mindset has a significant impact on your personal growth and success.
3. Define a fixed mindset and a growth mindset.
4. How can a fixed mindset hinder personal growth?
5. Give an example of a situation where a growth mindset can lead to better outcomes.
6. **True or False**: Mindset is a static trait and cannot be changed.
7. What are some strategies discussed in this section for developing a growth mindset?
8. How does a positive mindset influence your ability to overcome challenges?
9. What role does self-belief play in shaping your mindset?
10. Explain the concept of neuroplasticity and its connection to mindset.

Exercises for Section I.A: The Power of Mindset: Setting the Stage for Personal Growth

» **Mindset Reflection:** *Take a few moments each day to reflect on your thoughts and beliefs about your abilities and potential. Write down any fixed mindset thoughts that arise and challenge them by reframing them with a growth mindset perspective.*

» **Affirmation Practice:** *Create a list of positive affirmations that align with a growth mindset. Repeat these affirmations daily, emphasizing them with conviction and belief in your potential for growth and success.*

» **Success Stories Analysis:** *Study the success stories of individuals who have achieved great things despite facing significant challenges. Identify the mindset traits and attitudes they demonstrated on their journey and reflect on how you can apply those lessons to your own life.*

» **Visualization Exercise:** *Visualize yourself successfully overcoming a specific challenge or achieving a desired goal. Engage your senses, imagining the details of the situation, and experience the emotions associated with your accomplishment. This exercise* *reinforces a growth mindset by programming your mind for success.*

» **Reframing Obstacles:** *Choose a current challenge or obstacle you are facing. Write down three different ways to reframe it from a growth mindset perspective. Focus on seeing the opportunity for learning and growth embedded within the obstacle.*

» **Gratitude Journaling:** *Each day, write down three things you are grateful for related to your personal growth journey. Cultivate an appreciation for the progress you have made and the opportunities for growth that lie ahead. This practice enhances your mindset by emphasizing the positive aspects of your journey.*

» **Goal Setting:** *Set meaningful and achievable goals that align with your personal growth aspirations. Break them down into smaller milestones and create an action plan to move closer to their attainment. Regularly review and revise your goals as you make progress, reinforcing your growth mindset.*

» **Surround Yourself with Growth:** *Evaluate the people you surround yourself with and the content you consume. Seek out individuals, books, podcasts, or videos* *that inspire and support a growth mindset. Engage in conversations with others who share a similar mindset to foster mutual growth and encouragement.*

» **Mindset Accountability Buddy:** *Find an accountability partner who is also committed to personal growth. Share your goals, progress, and challenges with each other. Provide support, feedback, and motivation to foster a growth mindset in both yourself and your partner.*

» **Celebrate Small Wins:** *Acknowledge and celebrate your small victories along the personal growth journey. Recognize that progress is not always linear and that every step forward, no matter how small, contributes to your overall development.*

Quiz Answers for Section I.A: The Power of Mindset: Setting the Stage for Personal Growth

1. The main focus of Section I.A is exploring the power and impact of mindset on personal growth.
2. **True.** Your mindset significantly influences your personal growth and success.
3. A fixed mindset is the belief that abilities and intelligence are fixed traits, while a growth mindset is the belief that abilities and intelligence can be developed through effort, learning, and perseverance.
4. A fixed mindset can hinder personal growth by limiting one's willingness to take risks, learn from failures, and embrace challenges.
5. Answers may vary. **Example:** Embracing failure as an opportunity to learn and improve, rather than seeing it as a sign of inadequacy.
6. **False.** Mindset is not fixed and can be changed with awareness and intentional effort.
7. Strategies for developing a growth mindset include embracing challenges, seeking learning opportunities, persisting in the face of setbacks, and embracing the success of others.
8. A positive mindset enhances your ability to overcome challenges by fostering resilience, optimism, and a belief in your capacity to learn and grow.
9. Self-belief plays a crucial role in shaping your

mindset as it influences your motivation, willingness to take risks, and resilience in the face of obstacles.

10. Neuroplasticity refers to the brain's ability to adapt and reorganize itself by forming new neural connections. It is linked to mindset as it suggests that the brain can change and grow throughout life, supporting the development of a growth mindset.

Understanding the Mind-Body Connection

Welcome to the second part of our transformative journey. In this section, we will delve into the fascinating realm of the mind-body connection and explore the profound influence it holds over our well-being and personal growth. Prepare to unlock the secrets of this intricate relationship and harness its power to propel you toward lasting success and fulfillment.

The Mind-Body Connection: A Holistic Perspective

The mind and body are not separate entities but interconnected aspects of our being. They dance together in perfect harmony, influencing and shaping each other in profound ways. Understanding the mind-body connection is crucial for unleashing your inner potential and achieving holistic well-being. By recognizing the intricate interplay between your thoughts, emotions, beliefs, and physical state, you can harness this connection to optimize your personal growth journey.

The Power of Thoughts: Shaping Your Reality

Your thoughts have a remarkable ability to shape your reality. They are like seeds planted in the fertile soil of your mind, which, when nurtured, grow into the experiences and outcomes you manifest in your life. Each thought carries a vibrational frequency that reverberates throughout your being and interacts with the energy of the universe. When you cultivate positive, empowering thoughts, you attract corresponding experiences and opportunities. Conversely, negative thoughts can hinder your progress and limit your potential. By becoming aware of your thought patterns and consciously choosing thoughts aligned with your aspirations, you can transform your reality from the inside out.

Emotions as Messengers: Navigating the Inner Landscape

Emotions are the language of the soul, the messengers that convey important information about our inner state. They provide valuable insights into our needs, desires, and areas that require attention and healing. Rather than suppressing or avoiding emotions, it is essential to develop emotional intelligence and learn how to navigate the vast spectrum of human feelings. By cultivating emotional awareness and embracing our emotions with compassion and curiosity, we can gain profound wisdom, deepen our self-understanding, and harness the transformative power they hold. Emotions can serve as catalysts for personal growth, providing opportunities for healing, growth, and self-empowerment.

The Body as a Temple: Nurturing Your Physical Well-being

Your body is the vessel that carries you through life's journey. It is a sacred temple that deserves care, respect, and nourishment. Your physical well-being plays a pivotal role in supporting your mental, emotional, and spiritual growth. By adopting a holistic approach to self-care, you honor the mind-body connection and create a solid foundation for personal transformation. Engage in regular physical exercise, prioritize restful sleep, nourish your body with wholesome foods, and cultivate practices that promote relaxation and stress reduction. Embrace the harmony between your mind and body, and witness the synergistic effects on your overall well-being.

Mindfulness: The Gateway to Presence and Alignment

In the fast-paced modern world, it is easy to get caught up in the whirlwind of thoughts, distractions, and external demands. However, true personal growth requires presence and alignment with the present moment. Mindfulness is the practice of cultivating awareness of the present moment without judgment. It allows you to fully engage with your experiences, thoughts, and emotions, fostering a deep connection with your inner wisdom. By incorporating mindfulness into your daily life, you can tap into the power of the mind-body connection, experience greater clarity, and make conscious choices that align with your authentic self.

As we explore the intricacies of the mind-body connection, remember that your thoughts, emotions, and physical state are intricately intertwined. By nurturing a harmonious relationship between your mind and body, you lay the foundation for profound personal growth and transformation. Embrace this journey of self-discovery and leverage the power of the mind-body connection to unlock your true potential and create a life of lasting success and fulfillment.

Continue reading as we embark on the next part of our transformative adventure, where we delve into the art of identifying limiting beliefs and self-sabotaging patterns, empowering you to break free from the shackles that hinder your progress and unleash the full force of your inner potential.

Quiz Questions for Section I.B: Understanding the Mind-Body Connection

11. What is the main focus of Section I.B?
12. **True or False**: The mind and body are interconnected and influence each other.
13. Explain how stress impacts the mind and body.
14. How can practicing mindfulness enhance the mind-body connection?
15. Name two techniques discussed in this section for managing stress.
16. **True or False**: Developing a strong mind-body connection can improve overall well-being and resilience.
17. Describe the concept of psychosomatic symptoms and provide an example.
18. How does exercise contribute to a healthy mind-body connection?
19. In what ways can negative thoughts or emotions affect the body?
20. Explain the role of self-awareness in understanding the mind-body connection.

Exercises for Section I.B: Understanding the Mind-Body Connection

» **Body Scan Meditation:** *Set aside 10 minutes each day to practice a body scan meditation. Start from your toes and gradually move upward, paying attention to each body part and noticing any sensations or areas of tension. This exercise promotes awareness of the mind-body connection.*

» **Mindful Eating:** *Choose one meal each day to eat mindfully. Slow down and savor each bite, paying attention to the flavors, textures, and sensations in your body. Notice how your body responds to different foods and how your emotions may affect your eating experience.*

» **Breathing Techniques:** *Learn and practice different breathing techniques such as deep belly breathing, box breathing, or alternate nostril breathing. Use these techniques whenever you feel stressed or overwhelmed to bring your attention back to the present moment and regulate your mind-body connection.*

» **Progressive Muscle Relaxation:** *Find a comfortable position and systematically tense* *and relax each muscle group in your body, starting from your toes and working your way up to your head. This exercise promotes relaxation and awareness of tension held in the body.*

» **Movement and Mindfulness:** *Engage in a mindful movement practice such as yoga, tai chi, or qigong. Pay attention to the sensations, breath, and alignment of your body as you move. Notice the connection between your physical movements and your mental state.*

» **Journaling:** *Write in a journal to explore and reflect on the mind-body connection. Observe how your emotions, thoughts, and physical sensations are interconnected. Write down any patterns or insights you discover.*

» **Gratitude Walk:** *Take a walk in nature and practice gratitude as you observe your surroundings. Notice the sensations in your body, the beauty of nature, and the positive emotions that arise. Express gratitude for your body's ability to experience and connect with the world.*

» **Body Awareness Check-In:** *Throughout the day, pause and take a moment to check in with your body. Notice any areas of tension, discomfort, or relaxation. Take a few deep* *breaths and consciously release any physical or mental tension you may be holding.*

» **Mindful Stretching:** *Dedicate a few minutes each day to engage in gentle stretching exercises. Pay attention to the sensations in your muscles, joints, and breath as you move through each stretch. Connect with your body and cultivate a sense of relaxation and flexibility.*

» **Visualization Practice:** *Close your eyes and imagine yourself in a peaceful and serene place. Visualize your mind and body as connected and in harmony. Engage your senses to fully immerse yourself in the experience and reinforce the mind-body connection.*

Quiz Answers for Section I.B: Understanding the Mind-Body Connection

11. The main focus of Section I.B is exploring the interconnectedness between the mind and body.
12. **True.** The mind and body are intricately linked and influence each other.
13. Stress can impact the mind and body by triggering physical symptoms such as headaches, muscle tension, and digestive issues, as well as affecting mental well-being, leading to anxiety, irritability, and difficulty concentrating.
14. Practicing mindfulness enhances the mind-body connection by cultivating present-moment awareness, allowing individuals to observe and regulate their thoughts, emotions, and physical sensations with non-judgmental acceptance.
15. Examples of stress management techniques discussed in this section include deep breathing exercises, progressive muscle relaxation, and engaging in physical activities or hobbies that promote relaxation and well-being.
16. **True.** Developing a strong mind-body connection can improve overall well-being and resilience by enabling individuals to better understand and respond to their physical and emotional needs.

17. Psychosomatic symptoms refer to physical symptoms that arise or are influenced by psychological factors. For example, stress or anxiety may manifest as headaches, backaches, or stomachaches without an underlying physical cause.
18. Exercise contributes to a healthy mind-body connection by releasing endorphins, reducing stress hormones, improving sleep quality, and promoting overall physical and mental well-being.
19. Negative thoughts or emotions can affect the body by triggering physical responses such as increased heart rate, muscle tension, shallow breathing, and weakened immune system, among others.
20. Self-awareness plays a crucial role in understanding the mind-body connection as it allows individuals to observe and recognize the influence of their thoughts, emotions, and behaviors on their physical sensations and overall well-being.

II. Unleashing Your Inner Potential

Identifying Limiting Beliefs and Self-Sabotaging Patterns

Welcome to the second part of our transformative journey, where we dive deep into the realm of unleashing your inner potential. In this section, we will explore the powerful process of identifying and overcoming limiting beliefs and self-sabotaging patterns that hinder your growth and hold you back from reaching your true potential. Prepare to embark on a profound journey of self-discovery and liberation as we unravel the chains that bind you and set the stage for limitless possibilities.

The Power of Beliefs: Unveiling Your Inner Landscape

Beliefs shape the very fabric of our reality. They are the lens through which we perceive ourselves, others, and the world around us. Often, our beliefs are formed in our early years, influenced by our upbringing, experiences, and societal conditioning. While some beliefs empower us and propel us forward, others act as invisible barriers, limiting our potential and keeping us stuck in a cycle of self-doubt and self-sabotage.

To begin the process of identifying limiting beliefs, we must first bring them to the forefront of our awareness. Take a moment to reflect on the areas of your life where you feel stuck, where you find yourself repeating patterns that hinder your progress. These patterns often stem from deep-rooted beliefs that no longer serve you. They may manifest as thoughts like "I'm not good enough," "I don't deserve success," or "I'm always destined to fail." By shining a light on these beliefs, you can begin to challenge their validity and create space for new, empowering beliefs to take root.

Unmasking Self-Sabotaging Patterns: Breaking Free from the Cycle

Self-sabotage is the silent enemy that undermines our efforts and prevents us from fully realizing our potential. It is the voice in our head that whispers doubt and fear, convincing us that we are unworthy of success or incapable of achieving our goals. Self-sabotaging patterns can manifest in various ways, such as procrastination, fear of failure, perfectionism, or negative self-talk. They keep us trapped in our comfort zones, preventing us from taking bold steps forward and embracing the unknown.

To break free from self-sabotage, we must first become aware of our patterns. Notice the moments when you feel resistance, when you find yourself engaging in behaviors that hinder your progress. Pay attention to the excuses you make, the fears that arise, and the self-imposed limitations that hold you back. By shining a light on these patterns, you can reclaim your power and consciously choose a different path.

The Empowering Shift: Cultivating a Growth Mindset

Identifying limiting beliefs and self-sabotaging patterns is not meant to condemn or criticize ourselves. On the contrary, it is an empowering process of self-awareness that opens the door to growth and transformation. With this newfound awareness, we have the opportunity to cultivate a growth mindset—a mindset that embraces challenges, sees failures as stepping stones to success, and believes in the power of continuous learning and improvement.

A growth mindset is rooted in the belief that our abilities and intelligence can be developed through dedication, effort, and resilience. It is the understanding that setbacks are not permanent roadblocks but temporary detours on the path to success. By adopting a growth mindset, we shift our perspective from fixed limitations to infinite possibilities. We embrace challenges as opportunities for growth, view failures as valuable lessons, and approach life with curiosity, determination, and a belief in our capacity to evolve.

As you embark on the journey of identifying limiting beliefs and self-sabotaging patterns, remember that it is a process of self-discovery and liberation. It requires courage, vulnerability, and a willingness to challenge the narratives that have held you back. By uncovering and releasing these barriers, you pave the way for a new chapter in your life—one where you can fully unleash your inner potential and create a future filled with boundless opportunities.

Continue reading as we delve deeper into the art of cultivating a growth mindset, where we will explore practical strategies and techniques to embrace challenges and failures, and harness the power of visualization and affirmations to manifest your dreams and aspirations. Get ready to embark on a transformative journey of self-empowerment and personal growth.

Quiz Questions for Section II.A: Identifying Limiting Beliefs and Self-Sabotaging Patterns

21. What is the main focus of Section II.A?
22. **True or False**: Limiting beliefs are thoughts or beliefs that hold you back from reaching your full potential.
23. Why is it important to identify and challenge limiting beliefs?
24. Name two common examples of limiting beliefs.
25. How can self-reflection help in uncovering self-sabotaging patterns?
26. **True or False**: Limiting beliefs are permanent and cannot be changed.
27. Explain the concept of cognitive restructuring and how it can help overcome limiting beliefs.
28. What role does self-awareness play in identifying and transforming limiting beliefs?
29. Describe one technique or exercise discussed in this section for challenging and reframing limiting beliefs.
30. How can seeking support from others be beneficial in addressing limiting beliefs?

Exercises for Section II.A: Identifying Limiting Beliefs and Self-Sabotaging Patterns

» **Thought Record:** *Keep a journal and write down any negative or limiting thoughts that arise throughout the day. Challenge those thoughts by providing evidence against them and reframing them into more empowering and supportive beliefs.*

» **Belief Inventory:** *Make a list of your beliefs about yourself, your abilities, and your potential. Identify any beliefs that may be limiting or self-sabotaging. Choose one belief at a time to examine and challenge, replacing it with a more empowering belief.*

» **Visualization and Affirmations:** *Engage in visualization exercises where you imagine yourself successfully overcoming challenges and achieving your goals. Pair these visualizations with affirmations that counteract limiting beliefs and reinforce positive self-beliefs.*

» **Supportive Self-Talk:** *Practice using positive and supportive self-talk throughout the day. When you notice a negative thought or self-sabotaging pattern, consciously replace it with a supportive and empowering* *statement.*

- **Role Modeling:** *Identify individuals who have achieved what you aspire to accomplish or who possess qualities you admire. Study their stories and behaviors, and use them as inspiration to challenge and transcend your own limiting beliefs.*

- **Accountability Buddy:** *Find an accountability partner or join a supportive community where you can share your goals, progress, and challenges. Engage in regular check-ins to hold each other accountable and provide encouragement.*

- **Fear-Setting Exercise:** *Identify a fear or limiting belief that is holding you back. Write down the worst-case scenario and the potential benefits of taking action despite that fear. This exercise helps reframe fears and encourages taking calculated risks.*

- **Empowering Environment:** *Surround yourself with people, books, podcasts, or other resources that inspire and uplift you. Create an environment that fosters positivity, growth, and support in challenging and transforming limiting beliefs.*

- **Visualization Collage:** *Create a vision board or visualization collage using images,* *quotes, and affirmations that represent your desired beliefs and outcomes. Display it in a prominent place as a daily reminder of your aspirations and potential.*

» **Journaling Prompts:** *Use journaling prompts to explore and challenge limiting beliefs. For example, "What would I do if I believed I couldn't fail?" or "What evidence do I have that contradicts this limiting belief?" Write your responses with honesty and curiosity.*

Quiz Answers for Section II.A: Identifying Limiting Beliefs and Self-Sabotaging Patterns

21. The main focus of Section II.A is to explore and identify limiting beliefs and self-sabotaging patterns.
22. **True.** Limiting beliefs are thoughts or beliefs that hold you back from reaching your full potential.
23. It is important to identify and challenge limiting beliefs because they can significantly impact self-confidence, motivation, and actions. By recognizing and addressing them, individuals can unlock their true potential and pursue their goals with greater clarity and determination.
24. Examples of common limiting beliefs include "I'm not smart enough," "I don't deserve success," "I'm too old/young," "I'll never be good at [insert skill or activity]," etc.
25. Self-reflection helps uncover self-sabotaging patterns by encouraging individuals to examine their thoughts, behaviors, and outcomes. By analyzing past experiences, triggers, and patterns, one can identify recurring self-sabotage and work toward overcoming it.
26. **False.** Limiting beliefs are not permanent and can be changed through conscious effort and practice.
27. Cognitive restructuring involves challenging

and reframing limiting beliefs by examining the evidence supporting or contradicting them By questioning the validity of limiting beliefs and replacing them with more empowering alternatives, individuals can change their mindset and behavior.

28. Self-awareness plays a crucial role in identifying and transforming limiting beliefs. By becoming aware of one's thoughts, emotions, and behavioral patterns, individuals can recognize when limiting beliefs arise and consciously choose to challenge and change them.

29. One technique for challenging limiting beliefs is the ABCDE method: A - Identify the activating event, B - Examine the belief triggered by the event, C - Explore the consequences of that belief, D - Dispute the belief by providing evidence against it, and E - Establish a new, empowering belief.

30. Seeking support from others can be beneficial in addressing limiting beliefs because external perspectives, encouragement, and feedback can provide insights, alternative viewpoints, and accountability. Supportive relationships and communities can offer guidance, motivation, and reassurance throughout the process of transforming limiting beliefs.

Cultivating a Growth Mindset: Embracing Challenges and Failures

In our journey of unleashing your inner potential, one of the most transformative and empowering mindsets you can adopt is a growth mindset. A growth mindset is the belief that our abilities and intelligence can be developed through dedication, effort, and resilience. It is the understanding that challenges and failures are not indicators of our worth or fixed limitations but rather opportunities for growth, learning, and personal evolution. By cultivating a growth mindset, you can navigate the ups and downs of life with a sense of resilience, optimism, and a deep belief in your own potential.

Embracing Challenges: A Gateway to Growth

Challenges are not obstacles to be avoided; they are gateways to personal growth and self-discovery. When you embrace challenges with a growth mindset, you shift your perspective from seeing them as insurmountable hurdles to viewing them as opportunities for expansion and development. Challenges push you outside your comfort zone, forcing you to tap into your inner reserves of strength, creativity, and problem-solving skills. They provide you with the chance to stretch your limits, acquire new knowledge and skills, and uncover hidden strengths and abilities you may not have known existed.

To embrace challenges effectively, it is crucial to reframe your mindset. Instead of fearing failure or seeking immediate perfection, approach challenges as valuable learning experiences. Recognize that even if you stumble along the way, each step you take is an opportunity to grow stronger and wiser. Embrace the process of learning and improvement, celebrating small victories and using setbacks as springboards for further progress. Remember, it is through challenges that you refine your skills, deepen your understanding, and unlock your true potential.

Learning from Failures: Building Resilience and Gaining Wisdom

Failure is an inevitable part of any journey towards success. However, the way you perceive and respond to failure can make all the difference in your growth and development. In a growth mindset, failure is not viewed as a reflection of your worth or a permanent setback; rather, it is seen as a stepping stone on the path to success. It is an opportunity to learn, adjust, and persevere.

When faced with failure, it is essential to embrace a compassionate and growth-oriented mindset. Instead of dwelling on self-criticism or succumbing to negative self-talk, approach failure with curiosity and self-reflection. Ask yourself, "What can I learn from this experience? How can I improve next time?" By shifting your focus from self-judgment to self-improvement, you open the door to valuable insights and personal growth.

Moreover, building resilience is a fundamental aspect of cultivating a growth mindset. Resilience allows you to bounce back from setbacks, adapt to change, and persevere in the face of adversity. It is the inner strength that enables you to rise above challenges, maintain a positive outlook, and continue striving towards your goals.

To build resilience, practice self-compassion and self-care. Treat yourself with kindness and understanding, acknowledging that setbacks are a natural part of the journey. Engage in activities that recharge your energy, such as meditation, exercise, journaling, or spending time in nature. Surround yourself with a support system of positive and encouraging individuals who believe in your potential and can offer guidance and encouragement along the way.

Developing a growth mindset requires consistent effort and practice. Here are some strategies to help you cultivate and reinforce a growth-oriented perspective:

» **Embrace the Power of Yet:** *Replace statements like "I can't do it" with "I can't* *do it yet." This subtle shift acknowledges that with time, effort, and a growth mindset, you can develop the necessary skills and achieve your goals.*

» **Embrace the Unknown:** *Step outside your comfort zone and embrace new challenges and opportunities. Embracing the unknown allows you to expand your horizons, discover new passions, and develop a deeper understanding of your capabilities.*

» **Cultivate a Learning Attitude:** *Adopt a lifelong learner mindset, where every experience is an opportunity for growth and knowledge. Approach each day with curiosity, seeking to learn something new and embracing new perspectives.*

» **Practice Positive Self-Talk:** *Challenge negative thoughts and self-limiting beliefs by replacing them with positive and empowering affirmations. Remind yourself of your strengths, past successes, and the potential for growth and improvement.*

» **Set Realistic Goals:** *Break down your larger goals into smaller, achievable milestones. Celebrate each milestone you reach, as it signifies progress and reinforces your belief in your ability to overcome challenges.*

- **Seek Feedback and Support:** *Surround yourself with individuals who inspire and motivate you. Seek feedback from mentors, coaches, or trusted friends and family members who can provide guidance, constructive criticism, and encouragement.*

By adopting a growth mindset and embracing challenges and failures as opportunities for growth, you can unlock your true potential and achieve lasting success. Remember, the journey to self-mastery is not about perfection but progress. Embrace the process, stay resilient, and cultivate a mindset that empowers you to overcome any obstacle on your path to unleashing your inner potential.

Continue reading as we explore the art of visualization and affirmations, powerful techniques that can accelerate your personal growth and help you manifest your deepest desires and aspirations.

Quiz Questions for Section II.B: Cultivating a Growth Mindset: Embracing Challenges and Failures

31. What is the main focus of Section II.B?
32. Define a growth mindset and contrast it with a fixed mindset.
33. **True or False**: Embracing challenges and failures is essential for personal growth.
34. How does a growth mindset impact one's response to setbacks and obstacles?
35. What are some strategies discussed in this section for cultivating a growth mindset?
36. Explain the concept of reframing failure and its role in personal development.
37. Give an example of a situation where someone with a growth mindset would respond differently from someone with a fixed mindset.
38. How can celebrating small victories contribute to the development of a growth mindset?
39. **True or False**: Cultivating a growth mindset means ignoring one's limitations and setting unrealistic goals.
40. How can self-compassion support the cultivation of a growth mindset?

Exercises for Section II.B: Cultivating a Growth Mindset: Embracing Challenges and Failures

- » **Growth Mindset Journal:** *Write in a journal daily, reflecting on your experiences with challenges and failures. Describe how you approached them, what you learned, and how you can apply those lessons to future endeavors.*

- » **Obstacle Course:** *Create an obstacle course with various challenges, both physical and mental. Engage in the course regularly, pushing yourself to overcome obstacles and embracing the opportunity to learn and grow from each challenge.*

- » **Growth Mindset Affirmations:** *Create a list of positive affirmations that reinforce a growth mindset. Repeat these affirmations daily, especially when faced with challenges or setbacks, to reinforce your belief in your ability to learn and improve.*

- » **Failure Reflection:** *Choose a recent failure or setback and reflect on it. Write down what you learned from the experience, how it contributed to your personal growth, and how you can apply those lessons in the future.*

- » **Mentorship and Feedback:** *Seek out a mentor or coach who can provide guidance and feedback on your goals and progress. Embrace their constructive criticism and use it as an opportunity to grow and develop.*

- » **Embracing Discomfort:** *Step outside of your comfort zone and engage in activities or experiences that challenge you. Whether it's public speaking, trying a new hobby, or learning a new skill, embracing discomfort fosters growth and cultivates a growth mindset.*

- » **Growth Mindset Book Club:** *Start or join a book club focused on personal growth and mindset. Choose books that explore the concepts of resilience, embracing challenges, and developing a growth mindset. Discuss the ideas and insights with fellow members.*

- » **Learning from Role Models:** *Identify individuals who exemplify a growth mindset and have achieved success in their fields. Study their journeys, interviews, or biographies to gain inspiration and insights into their mindset and approach to challenges.*

- » **Visualization and Goal Setting:** *Visualize yourself successfully overcoming challenges and achieving your goals. Set specific,* *realistic goals that align with your growth mindset and create an action plan to work toward them.*

» **Gratitude Practice:** *Practice gratitude by keeping a gratitude journal or engaging in gratitude exercises. Recognize and appreciate the lessons and growth opportunities presented by challenges and failures.*

Quiz Answers for Section II.B: Cultivating a Growth Mindset: Embracing Challenges and Failures

31. The main focus of Section II.B is cultivating a growth mindset and embracing challenges and failures.

32. A growth mindset is the belief that abilities and intelligence can be developed through effort, practice, and learning. In contrast, a fixed mindset is the belief that abilities are fixed traits and cannot be significantly changed.

33. **True.** Embracing challenges and failures is essential for personal growth because they provide opportunities to learn, improve, and develop new skills.

34. A growth mindset allows individuals to see setbacks and obstacles as opportunities for learning and improvement. Instead of giving up, they persevere, adapt, and find alternative solutions.

35. Some strategies for cultivating a growth mindset include reframing challenges as opportunities, seeking feedback and constructive criticism, embracing the learning process, setting realistic goals, and practicing self-reflection and self-compassion.

36. Reframing failure involves viewing failures as learning experiences and opportunities for growth rather than personal shortcomings. It involves shifting the perspective from a

negative outcome to a chance for improvement and resilience.

37. **Example:** When faced with a difficult project, someone with a growth mindset would approach it with enthusiasm, see it as a chance to learn and improve, and embrace the challenges it presents. In contrast, someone with a fixed mindset might feel overwhelmed, avoid taking risks, and believe that their abilities are limited.

38. Celebrating small victories reinforces a growth mindset by acknowledging progress and achievements along the journey. It boosts motivation, confidence, and resilience.

39. **False.** Cultivating a growth mindset involves recognizing and accepting limitations while understanding that they can be improved with effort and practice. It is about setting realistic goals that stretch your abilities without being unrealistic or unattainable.

40. Self-compassion supports the cultivation of a growth mindset by fostering kindness, understanding, and acceptance toward oneself, even in the face of challenges or failures. It allows for learning from mistakes and encourages self-improvement without self-judgment or harsh criticism.

The Art of Visualization and Affirmations

In our quest to unleash your inner potential and cultivate a growth mindset, we delve into the transformative power of visualization and affirmations. These practices harness the innate capabilities of your mind to shape your reality, overcome challenges, and manifest your deepest desires. By incorporating the art of visualization and affirmations into your daily life, you can create a powerful synergy between your thoughts, beliefs, and actions, propelling you towards lasting success and personal fulfillment.

Visualization: Painting Your Path to Success

Visualization is a practice that involves creating vivid mental images of your desired outcomes and experiences. It taps into the immense power of your imagination to bring your goals and aspirations to life. When you engage in visualization, you create a detailed and multisensory representation of what you want to achieve or become. By repeatedly and intensely imagining these scenarios, you activate your subconscious mind and align your thoughts and actions with your desired reality.

To begin practicing visualization, find a quiet and comfortable space where you can relax and focus without distractions. Close your eyes and take several deep breaths, allowing yourself to enter a state of deep relaxation. Now, imagine yourself in the specific situation or achieving the desired outcome. Engage all your senses to make the visualization as vivid as possible. See the details, hear the sounds, feel the textures, and experience the emotions associated with your envisioned success.

While visualizing, pay attention to the positive emotions and sensations that arise within you. Let them amplify your motivation, belief, and confidence in your ability to achieve your goals. As you consistently engage in visualization, you create a mental blueprint that guides your subconscious mind towards taking the necessary actions to turn your visions into reality. Remember, visualization is not merely wishful thinking; it is a powerful tool that prepares your mind for success and primes you to recognize and seize opportunities that align with your aspirations.

Affirmations: Empowering Your Inner Dialogue

Affirmations are positive, empowering statements that you repeat to yourself consciously and consistently. They serve as a way to reprogram your subconscious mind and replace self-limiting beliefs and negative self-talk with uplifting and supportive thoughts. Affirmations are a form of self-talk that helps you align your conscious and subconscious mind, boosting your confidence, self-belief, and motivation.

To create effective affirmations, start by identifying the specific areas or aspects of your life where you want to experience positive change or growth. Then, craft affirmations that reflect the desired state you wish to manifest. For example, if you seek financial abundance, you can repeat affirmations such as "I am worthy of wealth and abundance," "I attract financial opportunities into my life," or "I am capable of creating wealth in a way that aligns with my values."

To maximize the impact of affirmations, incorporate the following strategies:

» **Use the present tense:** *Phrase your affirmations as if you have already achieved the desired outcome. This sends a powerful signal to your subconscious mind, reinforcing your belief in the present reality of your aspirations.*

» **Be specific and detailed:** *Clearly define what you want to manifest. Specific affirmations create a clear mental image and help you focus your intention and energy towards your goals.*

» **Use positive language:** *State your affirmations in positive terms, emphasizing what you want to attract or become. Avoid* *negative or restrictive words that can reinforce self-doubt or limitations.*

» **Repeat with conviction and emotion:** *Recite your affirmations with intention, passion, and belief. Engage your emotions and let the positive energy flow through your words and thoughts.*

Incorporate visualization and affirmations into your daily routine. Dedicate a few minutes each day to visualize your goals and repeat your affirmations. You can do this in the morning as a powerful way to set your intentions for the day or in the evening to reinforce positive thoughts and beliefs before sleep.

Remember that consistency and repetition are key. The more you practice visualization and affirmations, the more deeply embedded they become in your subconscious mind. Over time, these practices will help you overcome self-doubt, silence your inner critic, and align your thoughts, beliefs, and actions with the limitless potential within you.

As you explore the realm of visualization and affirmations, prepare to embark on a profound journey of self-discovery and transformation. In the upcoming sections, we will delve deeper into mastering your thoughts and emotions, and the power of gratitude and positivity, equipping you with the tools to overcome obstacles, embrace resilience, and unlock your true potential. Continue reading, and let the power of your mindset propel you towards lasting success.

Quiz Questions for Section II.C: The Art of Visualization and Affirmations

41. What is the main topic of Section II.C?
42. Define visualization and explain its role in mindset mastery.
43. **True or False**: Affirmations are positive statements that can help reprogram negative beliefs and foster a growth mindset.
44. How can visualization and affirmations work together to support personal growth?
45. What are some practical techniques for incorporating visualization into daily practice?
46. Give an example of how visualization can be used to overcome challenges or achieve goals.
47. How can affirmations be tailored to address specific limiting beliefs or self-sabotaging patterns?
48. **True or False**: Visualization and affirmations are only effective if done passively without taking action.
49. What role does emotion play in the effectiveness of visualization and affirmations?
50. How can visualization and affirmations help in maintaining focus and motivation during challenging times?

Exercises for Section II.C: The Art of Visualization and Affirmations

- **Vision Board Creation:** *Create a vision board by collecting images, words, and quotes that represent your goals, aspirations, and desired mindset. Display the vision board in a prominent place as a daily reminder of your aspirations.*

- **Guided Visualization Meditation:** *Find a guided visualization meditation online or through a meditation app. Set aside dedicated time each day to listen to the guided meditation, allowing yourself to immerse in positive imagery and emotions.*

- **Morning Affirmation Ritual:** *Develop a morning affirmation ritual where you repeat empowering affirmations related to your goals, mindset, and self-worth. Say them out loud, with conviction, in front of a mirror to reinforce positive self-beliefs.*

- **Mind Movie Creation:** *Use technology or software to create a short video that incorporates images, music, and affirmations that align with your desired mindset and goals. Watch the mind movie regularly to reinforce positive visual and auditory stimuli.*

- **Visualization Journaling:** *Dedicate a*

journal specifically for visualization exercises Write detailed descriptions of your desired outcomes, imagining them vividly and incorporating sensory details. Revisit and revise your visualizations regularly.

» **Positive Affirmation Jar:** *Fill a jar with small pieces of paper on which you've written positive affirmations. Each day, randomly select an affirmation from the jar and repeat it to yourself throughout the day, internalizing its message.*

» **Visualization Partners:** *Find a visualization accountability partner or group. Share your goals and visualizations with each other and provide mutual support, encouragement, and feedback.*

» **Future Self-Letter:** *Write a letter to your future self, describing the person you aspire to become and the mindset you want to embody. Reflect on this letter periodically to reinforce your commitment to personal growth.*

» **Affirmation Walk:** *Take a walk in a natural environment while repeating affirmations related to your goals, self-beliefs, and mindset. Engage your senses and connect with nature while reaffirming positive statements.*

» **Visualization Role Play:** *Enlist a trusted friend or family member to participate in a visualization role-play exercise. Take turns visualizing challenging scenarios and mentally rehearsing positive outcomes, providing support and feedback to each other.*

Quiz Answers for Section II.C: The Art of Visualization and Affirmations

41. The main topic of Section II.C is the art of visualization and affirmations.

42. Visualization is the practice of creating vivid mental imagery of desired outcomes, experiences, or goals. It plays a crucial role in mindset mastery by harnessing the power of the mind to align beliefs and actions with desired results.

43. **True.** Affirmations are positive statements that can help reprogram negative beliefs and reinforce desired thoughts and behaviors.

44. Visualization and affirmations work together by utilizing the power of the mind to create a clear mental image of desired outcomes (visualization) and reinforcing positive beliefs and self-talk (affirmations).

45. Practical techniques for incorporating visualization include creating a vision board, engaging in guided visualization meditations, and practicing visualization journaling.

46. An example could be visualizing yourself confidently giving a presentation and receiving applause and positive feedback from the audience.

47. Affirmations can be tailored by identifying specific limiting beliefs or self-sabotaging patterns and creating positive statements that counteract those beliefs or patterns.

48. **False.** Visualization and affirmations are

most effective when combined with action. They serve as tools to align the mind with desired outcomes and motivate action toward achieving them.

49. Emotion adds depth and intensity to visualization and affirmations, making them more impactful. When positive emotions are evoked during visualization and affirmation practice, they reinforce the desired mindset.

50. Visualization and affirmations help maintain focus and motivation during challenging times by reminding individuals of their goals, reinforcing positive beliefs, and providing a mental framework for overcoming obstacles.

III. Mastering Your Thoughts and Emotions

Taming the Inner Critic: Overcoming Negative Self-Talk

In our journey towards mastering our thoughts and emotions, one of the most crucial aspects is taming the inner critic—the voice within us that constantly judges, doubts, and undermines our self-worth. Negative self-talk can be pervasive, insidious, and detrimental to our well-being and personal growth. It creates barriers that hinder us from reaching our true potential and living a fulfilling life. However, by understanding the nature of our inner critic and developing effective strategies to overcome it, we can break free from its grip and cultivate a more compassionate and empowering internal dialogue.

The Nature of the Inner Critic

The inner critic is formed through a combination of our upbringing, societal conditioning, and past experiences. It is the voice that tells us we are not good enough, smart enough, or deserving of success. It magnifies our flaws, amplifies our self-doubt, and fills our minds with fear and self-criticism. The inner critic often emerges as a result of internalizing external judgments, comparisons, and expectations.

Recognizing Your Inner Critic

To overcome negative self-talk, it is essential to first recognize when our inner critic is active. The inner critic can manifest in various ways, such as:

- **Harsh self-judgment:** *When we excessively criticize ourselves, focus on our shortcomings, and magnify our mistakes while dismissing our achievements.*

- **Perfectionism:** *Setting unrealistic standards for ourselves and feeling inadequate or unworthy when we fail to meet them.*

- **Catastrophizing:** *Assuming the worst-case scenarios and anticipating failure or rejection in every situation.*

- **Comparison and envy:** *Constantly comparing ourselves to others, feeling inadequate in their presence, and resenting their successes.*

- **Self-sabotage:** *Engaging in behaviors that undermine our progress and success due to a lack of self-belief or fear of failure.*

Challenging and Overcoming the Inner Critic

Overcoming the inner critic requires a combination of self-awareness, self-compassion, and cognitive restructuring. Here are effective strategies to tame the inner critic and cultivate a more positive and empowering internal dialogue:

- **Awareness and mindfulness:** *Begin by developing awareness of your inner critic. Notice when negative self-talk arises and the impact it has on your emotions and behavior. Practice mindfulness to observe your thoughts without judgment, allowing them to pass without clinging to or believing them.*

- **Self-compassion:** *Replace self-judgment with self-compassion. Treat yourself with kindness, understanding, and acceptance, just as you would a close friend or loved one. Offer yourself words of encouragement and support in challenging moments.*

- **Cognitive reframing:** *Challenge the validity of your negative self-talk by questioning the evidence behind it. Look for alternative, more balanced perspectives and evidence that contradicts your self-critical thoughts. Replace negative statements with positive, realistic, and affirming ones.*

- **Empowering affirmations:** *Create a list of positive affirmations that counteract your specific self-critical beliefs. Repeat these affirmations daily to reprogram your subconscious mind and reinforce positive self-talk.*

- » **Journaling:** *Use journaling as a tool for self-reflection and exploration. Write down your self-critical thoughts and then objectively analyze them. Look for patterns, triggers, and underlying beliefs. Use your journal to challenge and reframe these negative thoughts.*

- » **Surround yourself with positive influences:** *Seek out supportive and encouraging relationships. Surround yourself with people who uplift and inspire you, and distance yourself from those who perpetuate negativity or trigger your inner critic.*

- » **Celebrate successes and strengths:** *Shift your focus from your perceived weaknesses to your strengths and accomplishments. Acknowledge and celebrate even the smallest victories, building confidence and self-belief along the way.*

- » **Seek professional support if needed:** *If your negative self-talk is deeply ingrained or significantly impacts your well-being, consider seeking the guidance of a therapist or counselor. They can provide valuable insights, tools, and techniques to help you overcome the inner critic.*

Remember, taming the inner critic is an ongoing process. It requires patience, self-compassion, and consiscent effort. As you develop the ability to recognize and challenge your negative self-talk, you will gradually cultivate a more supportive and empowering mindset. This transformation will pave the way for greater self-acceptance, personal growth, and a deeper connection with your authentic self. Embrace this journey and let go of the limiting beliefs that have held you back. The power to reshape your inner dialogue and unleash your true potential lies within you.

Quiz Questions for Section III.A: Taming the Inner Critic: Overcoming Negative Self-Talk

51. What is the main topic of Section III.A?
52. Define negative self-talk and explain its impact on personal growth.
53. **True or False**: The inner critic is always an accurate reflection of your abilities and worth.
54. What are some common triggers or situations that can activate the inner critic?
55. How does negative self-talk influence emotions, behavior, and mindset?
56. What are some strategies for recognizing and identifying negative self-talk patterns?
57. Explain the concept of cognitive reframing and how it can help overcome negative self-talk.
58. What role does self-compassion play in taming the inner critic?
59. How can mindfulness practices support the process of taming the inner critic?
60. What are some practical techniques for replacing negative self-talk with positive and empowering thoughts?

Exercises for Section III.A: Taming the Inner Critic: Overcoming Negative Self-Talk

» **Self-Talk Awareness Journaling:** *Keep a journal to record instances of negative self-talk throughout the day. Reflect on the underlying beliefs and emotions associated with each instance and identify patterns or triggers.*

» **Reframing Exercise:** *Take a negative self-talk statement and challenge it by finding evidence or alternative perspectives that contradict it. Write down the new, positive statement that reframes the initial negative thought.*

» **Mirror Work:** *Stand in front of a mirror and practice replacing negative self-talk with positive affirmations and compassionate self-talk. Engage in eye contact with yourself and speak affirming words aloud.*

» **The Inner Cheerleader:** *Imagine having an inner cheerleader, a positive and supportive voice inside your head. Whenever the inner critic arises, visualize the cheerleader offering encouragement and positive affirmations.*

» **Gratitude Shift:** *When negative self-talk*

arises, interrupt the pattern by shifting focus to gratitude. List three things you are grateful for related to yourself or the situation at hand to cultivate a positive mindset.

» **Thought-Stopping Technique:** *Whenever negative self-talk arises, say "stop" out loud or in your mind, then replace the negative thought with a positive or neutral affirmation. Practice this technique consistently to break the habit of negative self-talk.*

» **Power of Affirmations:** *Create a list of personalized positive affirmations that counteract your specific negative self-talk patterns. Repeat these affirmations daily, preferably in front of a mirror, to reinforce positive self-beliefs.*

» **Self-Compassion Letter:** *Write a compassionate letter to yourself, acknowledging your struggles, and offering words of understanding and self-compassion. Revisit this letter in moments of self-criticism to cultivate self-acceptance.*

» **Mindful Self-Reflection:** *Set aside dedicated time each day for self-reflection. Practice mindfulness techniques such as deep breathing and body scan meditation to cultivate awareness of negative self-talk and* *respond with self-compassion.*

- **Supportive Visualization:** *Engage in guided visualization exercises where you imagine a compassionate and supportive figure, such as a mentor or loved one, providing encouragement and reassurance when the inner critic arises.*

Quiz Answers for Section III.A: Taming the Inner Critic: Overcoming Negative Self-Talk

51. The main topic of Section III.A is taming the inner critic and overcoming negative self-talk.

52. Negative self-talk refers to the critical and self-defeating thoughts and beliefs individuals direct towards themselves. It can hinder personal growth by eroding self-confidence and reinforcing limiting beliefs.

53. **False.** The inner critic often distorts reality and tends to be overly harsh and critical, regardless of actual abilities and worth.

54. Common triggers for the inner critic include making mistakes, receiving criticism, comparison to others, and challenging situations that evoke self-doubt.

55. Negative self-talk can lead to negative emotions such as anxiety, shame, and self-doubt. It can also influence behavior by holding individuals back from taking risks or pursuing goals. Furthermore, negative self-talk perpetuates a negative mindset that reinforces limiting beliefs.

56. Strategies for recognizing negative self-talk patterns include self-awareness, observing thoughts without judgment, and identifying recurring themes or specific triggers.

57. Cognitive reframing involves consciously challenging and replacing negative thoughts with more realistic, positive, or balanced

perspectives. It helps reframe situations and beliefs in a way that is more empowering and supportive.

58. Self-compassion involves treating oneself with kindness, understanding, and acceptance, especially in the face of mistakes or shortcomings. It counteracts the harsh judgment of the inner critic and fosters self-care and resilience.

59. Mindfulness practices help tame the inner critic by increasing present-moment awareness, detaching from negative thoughts, and cultivating self-compassion. They create a mental space to observe thoughts and emotions without getting caught up in them.

60. Practical techniques for replacing negative self-talk include positive affirmations, cognitive restructuring, gratitude practices, seeking support from others, and engaging in self-care activities that boost self-esteem and well-being.

Emotional Intelligence: Navigating and Harnessing Emotions

Emotional intelligence is a fundamental skill in personal growth and overall well-being. It refers to the ability to recognize, understand, and manage our own emotions, as well as empathize with and effectively communicate with others. Developing emotional intelligence empowers us to navigate life's challenges, build meaningful relationships, and make sound decisions that align with our values and goals. In this section, we will explore the importance of emotional intelligence and provide practical strategies to enhance this crucial aspect of self-mastery.

Understanding Emotional Intelligence

Emotional intelligence encompasses several key components:

» **Self-awareness:** *This involves recognizing and understanding our own emotions, strengths, weaknesses, and triggers. Self-awareness allows us to gain insight into our emotional patterns and how they impact our thoughts and actions.*

» **Self-regulation:** *Self-regulation is the ability to manage and control our emotions, impulses, and reactions. It involves* *developing emotional resilience, practicing impulse control, and adapting to changing circumstances with composure and flexibility.*

» **Empathy:** *Empathy involves understanding and sharing the emotions of others. It enables us to connect with and relate to the experiences of those around us, fostering deeper understanding and compassion in our interactions.*

» **Social skills:** *Social skills encompass effective communication, active listening, conflict resolution, and collaboration. These skills enable us to build and nurture healthy relationships, work well in teams, and navigate social dynamics with empathy and respect.*

The Importance of Emotional Intelligence

Emotional intelligence plays a vital role in personal growth and success. Here are some key reasons why cultivating emotional intelligence is essential:

» **Self-awareness and self-management:** *Emotional intelligence allows us to understand our emotions and manage them effectively. By recognizing our emotional triggers, we can respond rather than react, make conscious choices, and avoid impulsive* *or destructive behavior.*

- **Improved relationships:** *Developing emotional intelligence enhances our ability to empathize with others, understand their perspectives, and communicate effectively. It strengthens our connections, resolves conflicts, and fosters healthier, more fulfilling relationships.*

- **Decision-making and problem-solving:** *Emotional intelligence helps us make informed decisions by considering both our emotions and rational thinking. It enables us to evaluate situations objectively, analyze potential consequences, and choose the most appropriate course of action.*

- **Resilience and adaptability:** *Emotional intelligence equips us with the tools to navigate challenges and setbacks. It allows us to bounce back from failures, manage stress effectively, and adapt to change with grace and resilience.*

- **Leadership and teamwork:** *Effective leadership requires emotional intelligence to inspire, motivate, and understand the needs of team members. It fosters a positive and supportive work environment, promotes collaboration, and enhances overall team performance.*

Developing Emotional Intelligence

Enhancing emotional intelligence is an ongoing process that requires self-reflection, practice, and a willingness to grow. Here are some strategies to cultivate emotional intelligence:

» **Cultivate self-awareness:** *Take time to reflect on your emotions, triggers, and patterns of behavior. Practice mindfulness and self-reflection to develop a deeper understanding of yourself.*

» **Practice emotional regulation:** *Learn techniques to manage your emotions effectively. Deep breathing, meditation, and journaling can help you gain control over intense emotions and maintain inner calm.*

» **Develop empathy:** *Seek to understand others' perspectives and emotions. Practice active listening, engage in compassionate communication, and put yourself in others' shoes to foster empathy and connection.*

» **Enhance social skills:** *Improve your communication skills, both verbal and nonverbal. Practice active listening, express yourself clearly and respectfully, and develop conflict resolution techniques.*

» **Seek feedback:** *Request feedback from trusted individuals to gain insights into how* *you are perceived and how your emotions impact others. Use feedback constructively to grow and improve your emotional intelligence.*

» **Learn from role models:** *Observe individuals with strong emotional intelligence and learn from their behaviors and approaches to emotional challenges. Model their strategies and adapt them to suit your own style.*

» **Practice emotional agility:** *Embrace change and uncertainty with an open mind. Develop the ability to adapt and respond flexibly to challenging situations, finding opportunities for growth and learning.*

Remember that developing emotional intelligence takes time and patience. Be kind to yourself throughout the process and celebrate small victories along the way. By cultivating emotional intelligence, you will enhance your personal and professional relationships, make wiser decisions, and experience greater fulfillment and success in all areas of life.

In the next section, we will explore the power of gratitude and positivity in transforming our mindset and creating a more fulfilling life.

Quiz Questions for Section III.B: Emotional Intelligence: Navigating and Harnessing Emotions

61. What is the main topic of Section III.B?
62. Define emotional intelligence and its significance in personal growth and relationships.
63. **True or False**: Emotional intelligence is a fixed trait and cannot be developed or improved.
64. Name and describe the five components of emotional intelligence.
65. How does emotional intelligence contribute to effective communication and conflict resolution?
66. What are some strategies for enhancing self-awareness, a key aspect of emotional intelligence?
67. Explain the concept of empathy and its role in nurturing relationships.
68. How can emotional intelligence help in managing stress and building resilience?
69. Discuss the importance of emotional regulation and provide techniques for practicing it.
70. How can emotional intelligence positively impact personal and professional success?

Exercises for Section III.B: Emotional Intelligence: Navigating and Harnessing Emotions

- » **Emotional Journaling:** *Keep a journal to record your emotions throughout the day. Reflect on the triggers, patterns, and physical sensations associated with different emotions. Identify strategies for effectively managing and expressing emotions.*

- » **The Emotional Wheel:** *Create a visual representation of the emotional wheel, which includes a wide range of emotions. Use this tool to identify and label your emotions accurately, increasing self-awareness of your emotional landscape.*

- » **Role-Play Scenarios:** *Engage in role-playing exercises where you practice recognizing and responding to different emotional cues in social interactions. This helps develop empathy and enhances emotional intelligence in real-life situations.*

- » **Mindful Emotion Check-Ins:** *Set aside dedicated moments throughout the day to check in with your emotions. Practice mindfulness techniques such as deep breathing and body scan meditation to observe and accept your emotions without* *judgment.*

- **Empathy Mapping:** *Choose a person in your life and create an empathy map for them. Consider their thoughts, feelings, needs, and motivations. This exercise fosters empathy and helps strengthen your understanding of others' emotions.*

- **Conflict Resolution Simulation:** *Simulate a conflict scenario with a partner or friend. Practice active listening, empathy, and effective communication techniques to navigate the conflict and find a resolution that considers both perspectives.*

- **Emotional Regulation Toolbox:** *Create an emotional regulation toolbox by identifying strategies that help you regulate and manage difficult emotions. This could include deep breathing exercises, visualization techniques, or engaging in hobbies that bring you joy.*

- **Emotional Intelligence Book Club:** *Start a book club or join an existing one focused on emotional intelligence and self-development. Read books that explore emotional intelligence concepts and discuss insights and personal experiences with other club members.*

- **Reflective Writing:** *Set aside time for reflective writing where you explore your emotional experiences, triggers, and patterns. Use prompts to delve deeper into your emotional landscape and gain insights into your emotional intelligence journey.*

- **Expressive Art Therapy:** *Engage in expressive art activities such as painting, drawing, or sculpting to explore and express your emotions. Let your emotions guide your creative process and reflect on the meaning behind your artwork.*

Quiz Answers for Section III.B: Emotional Intelligence: Navigating and Harnessing Emotions

61. The main topic of Section III.B is emotional intelligence and its role in personal growth and relationships.

62. Emotional intelligence refers to the ability to recognize, understand, and manage emotions, both in oneself and others. It is significant in personal growth as it enhances self-awareness, communication, empathy, and resilience.

63. **False.** Emotional intelligence is a learnable skill that can be developed and improved with practice and self-reflection.

64. The five components of emotional intelligence are self-awareness, self-regulation, motivation, empathy, and social skills.

65. Emotional intelligence contributes to effective communication and conflict resolution by promoting active listening, empathy, and understanding of others' perspectives. It helps manage emotions during challenging conversations and fosters better relationship dynamics.

66. Strategies for enhancing self-awareness include keeping an emotional journal, practicing mindfulness, seeking feedback from others, and reflecting on personal values and triggers.

67. Empathy is the ability to understand and share the feelings of another person. It plays

a crucial role in nurturing relationships by promoting understanding, compassion, and supportive communication.

68. Emotional intelligence helps in managing stress and building resilience by enabling individuals to recognize and regulate their emotions effectively. It allows for adaptive coping strategies, problem-solving, and maintaining a positive mindset in the face of challenges.

69. Emotional regulation involves the ability to manage and express emotions in a healthy and balanced way. Techniques for practicing emotional regulation include deep breathing, relaxation exercises, cognitive reframing, and seeking social support.

70. Emotional intelligence positively impacts personal and professional success by fostering effective leadership, teamwork, adaptability, and communication skills. It also contributes to emotional well-being, satisfaction, and healthier relationships.

The Power of Gratitude and Positivity

Gratitude and positivity are transformative forces that have the potential to shift our mindset, elevate our well-being, and create lasting success. In this section, we will explore the profound impact of gratitude and positivity on our thoughts, emotions, and overall outlook on life. We will delve into practical techniques and exercises to cultivate gratitude and foster a positive mindset, enabling us to unlock our true potential and experience greater fulfillment in our personal and professional lives.

Understanding Gratitude

Gratitude is the practice of recognizing and appreciating the goodness and blessings in our lives. It involves acknowledging the positive aspects, experiences, and relationships that we often take for granted. Gratitude shifts our focus from what is lacking to what we have, allowing us to develop a deeper sense of contentment and joy.

The Power of Gratitude

» **Shifts perspective:** *Gratitude helps us reframe our mindset by shifting our focus from negativity and scarcity to abundance and positivity. It allows us to see* *opportunities, blessings, and silver linings even in challenging situations.*

» **Enhances well-being:** *Research has shown that practicing gratitude regularly is associated with improved mental and physical well-being. It reduces stress, increases happiness, improves sleep quality, and boosts overall resilience.*

» **Strengthens relationships:** *Expressing gratitude fosters deeper connections and strengthens our relationships. When we appreciate and acknowledge others' kindness, support, and contributions, it enhances trust, empathy, and overall relationship satisfaction.*

» **Cultivates optimism:** *Gratitude nurtures a positive outlook on life. It helps us develop resilience in the face of adversity and encourages us to approach challenges with optimism and a growth mindset.*

Practicing Gratitude

» **Gratitude journaling:** *Set aside a few minutes each day to write down three things you are grateful for. Be specific and focus on the small moments, people, or experiences that brought you joy or made a positive impact.*

» **Gratitude letters:** *Write a heartfelt letter expressing your gratitude to someone who has made a significant difference in your life. Share how their actions or presence has influenced you and express your appreciation.*

» **Gratitude rituals:** *Create rituals that remind you to practice gratitude daily. It could be saying a gratitude prayer before meals, keeping a gratitude jar where you jot down moments of gratitude, or sharing gratitude with loved ones at the end of each day.*

» **Gratitude meditation:** *Incorporate gratitude into your mindfulness or meditation practice. Take a few moments to focus on what you are grateful for, allowing those feelings of appreciation to permeate your being.*

Fostering Positivity

Positivity is a state of mind characterized by optimism, hope, and a focus on the possibilities and potentials in life. It involves nurturing positive thoughts, emotions, and attitudes, even in the face of challenges. By cultivating positivity, we create a fertile ground for personal growth, resilience, and success.

The Power of Positivity

- » **Enhances resilience:** *Positive thinking enhances our ability to bounce back from setbacks and navigate obstacles with determination and resilience. It helps us view challenges as opportunities for growth and learning.*

- » **Boosts motivation:** *A positive mindset fuels motivation and drive. When we approach tasks and goals with positivity, we are more likely to persevere, take initiative, and maintain a proactive attitude.*

- » **Attracts opportunities:** *Positivity magnetizes opportunities and possibilities. It opens doors, expands our horizons, and attracts like-minded individuals who can support and collaborate with us on our journey.*

- » **Inspires others:** *Positivity is contagious. When we radiate positivity, we uplift and inspire those around us. Our positive attitude can have a ripple effect, creating a positive and supportive environment.*

Practicing Positivity

- » **Positive self-talk:** *Pay attention to your inner dialogue and replace self-limiting or negative thoughts with positive affirmations and statements. Encourage and support* *yourself with kind and empowering words.*

- **Surround yourself with positivity:** *Surround yourself with positive influences, whether it's uplifting books, inspiring podcasts, or supportive and optimistic individuals who encourage your personal growth and well-being.*

- **Gratitude and positivity integration:** *Integrate gratitude and positivity practices by starting your day with gratitude and setting positive intentions for the day. Carry that positivity throughout the day by noticing and appreciating the positive moments, achievements, and strengths.*

- **Visualization and affirmations:** *Utilize the power of visualization and affirmations to reinforce positive beliefs and outcomes. Imagine yourself succeeding, visualize your goals manifesting, and repeat positive affirmations that resonate with your aspirations.*

By cultivating gratitude and fostering positivity, we tap into the limitless potential within us and create a fertile ground for personal growth, happiness, and success. Practice gratitude and positivity consistently, and witness the transformative impact they have on your life.

In the next section, we will explore the importance of building resilience and taking action to overcome setbacks and challenges on our path to unleashing our inner potential.

Quiz Questions for Section III.C: The Power of Gratitude and Positivity

71. What is the main focus of Section III.C?
72. Define gratitude and explain its significance in personal growth and well-being.
73. How does practicing gratitude contribute to shifting one's mindset?
74. **True or False**: Gratitude is solely about focusing on positive aspects and ignoring challenges or negative experiences.
75. Name and describe three techniques for cultivating gratitude in daily life.
76. Discuss the benefits of incorporating a gratitude practice into your routine.
77. How can gratitude positively impact your relationships with others?
78. What is the relationship between gratitude and resilience?
79. Explain the concept of positive affirmations and their role in fostering positivity.
80. How can incorporating positive affirmations into your mindset contribute to achieving lasting success?

Exercises for Section III.C: The Power of Gratitude and Positivity

» **Gratitude Journaling:** *Start a gratitude journal where you write down three things you are grateful for each day. Reflect on why they bring you joy and how they enhance your life.*

» **Gratitude Letter:** *Write a heartfelt letter expressing your gratitude to someone who has had a positive impact on your life. Deliver or read the letter to them in person, if possible.*

» **Gratitude Walk:** *Take a walk in nature while focusing on gratitude. As you walk, notice and appreciate the beauty around you. Practice expressing gratitude for the sights, sounds, and sensations you experience.*

» **Random Acts of Kindness:** *Engage in random acts of kindness throughout your day. These acts can be as simple as holding the door for someone or offering a genuine compliment. Notice how expressing kindness makes you feel and its impact on others.*

» **Gratitude Meditation:** *Find a quiet space and engage in a gratitude meditation practice. Focus your attention on feelings of gratitude, visualizing people, experiences,* *or things you are grateful for. Allow these feelings to fill your mind and body.*

» **Gratitude Jar:** *Get a jar and small pieces of paper. Each day, write down one thing you are grateful for and put it in the jar. Over time, observe how the jar fills up, serving as a visual reminder of the abundance of things to be grateful for.*

» **Positive Affirmations Mirror Exercise:** *Stand in front of a mirror and practice saying positive affirmations to yourself. Repeat empowering statements about your abilities, strengths, and potential. Notice the impact of these affirmations on your self-perception.*

» **Gratitude Circle:** *Gather a group of friends or family members and create a gratitude circle. Each person takes turns expressing something they are grateful for. The exercise fosters connection, positivity, and appreciation for one another.*

» **Gratitude Collage:** *Create a gratitude collage using images and words from magazines or online sources. Select visuals that represent things you are grateful for in your life. Display the collage in a visible place as a reminder of gratitude.*

» **Gratitude Sharing on Social Media:**

Share moments of gratitude on social media platforms. Post about things you appreciate, acts of kindness you've witnessed, or express gratitude towards someone in your life. Encourage others to join in and spread positivity.

Quiz Answers for Section III.C: The Power of Gratitude and Positivity

71. The main focus of Section III.C is exploring the power of gratitude and positivity in personal growth.
72. Gratitude is the practice of recognizing and appreciating the positive aspects of life. It enhances well-being, shifts perspective, and fosters a sense of contentment and abundance.
73. Practicing gratitude contributes to shifting one's mindset by redirecting focus from what is lacking to what is present and positive. It helps cultivate a mindset of abundance and appreciation.
74. **False.** Gratitude acknowledges both positive and negative experiences, but it emphasizes shifting attention to the positive aspects and finding lessons or silver linings in challenges.
75. Three techniques for cultivating gratitude are keeping a gratitude journal, expressing gratitude to others, and practicing mindfulness and presence in daily activities.
76. Incorporating a gratitude practice into your routine enhances overall well-being, increases happiness, improves relationships, reduces stress, and fosters a positive mindset and resilience.
77. Gratitude positively impacts relationships by promoting appreciation, empathy, and kindness. It strengthens connections, fosters a supportive environment, and cultivates a sense

of gratitude between individuals.

78. Gratitude and resilience are closely linked. Gratitude practices help develop resilience by reframing challenges as opportunities for growth, promoting a positive mindset, and enhancing coping strategies during difficult times.

79. Positive affirmations are empowering statements that reflect desired qualities, goals, or beliefs. They reinforce positive self-perception, boost confidence, and support the development of a positive mindset.

80. Incorporating positive affirmations into your mindset can contribute to achieving lasting success by strengthening self-belief, fostering a growth mindset, enhancing motivation, and attracting opportunities aligned with your goals.

IV. Building Resilience and Taking Action

Developing Resilience: Bouncing Back from Setbacks

Resilience is the ability to adapt, recover, and bounce back from adversity, challenges, and setbacks. In this section, we will explore the importance of developing resilience on our journey to unleashing our inner potential. We will delve into the key elements of resilience, strategies to strengthen our resilience muscle, and techniques to navigate and overcome obstacles that come our way. By cultivating resilience, we empower ourselves to face life's challenges with courage, tenacity, and a growth mindset.

Understanding Resilience

Resilience is not an innate trait; it is a skill that can be cultivated and developed. It is the ability to persevere, stay strong, and maintain a sense of hope and optimism, even in the face of adversity. Resilience enables us to navigate setbacks, learn from failures, and emerge stronger and wiser.

The Elements of Resilience

» **Emotional resilience:** *Emotional resilience involves acknowledging and managing our emotions effectively, especially during challenging times. It requires developing self-awareness, regulating emotions, and* *cultivating a positive outlook.*

» **Mental resilience:** *Mental resilience refers to the ability to maintain clarity, focus, and mental strength in the face of obstacles. It involves developing a growth mindset, reframing negative thoughts, and nurturing self-belief and optimism.*

» **Social resilience:** *Social resilience emphasizes the importance of building and nurturing supportive relationships and networks. It involves seeking help, fostering connections, and cultivating empathy and effective communication.*

» **Physical resilience:** *Physical resilience involves taking care of our physical well-being, which includes adequate sleep, regular exercise, healthy nutrition, and practicing self-care. Physical well-being strengthens our overall resilience and ability to cope with stress.*

Strategies to Develop Resilience

» **Cultivate a growth mindset:** *Embrace challenges and failures as opportunities for growth and learning. Develop the belief that setbacks are temporary and that you have the capacity to overcome them and emerge stronger.*

- **Build a support system:** *Surround yourself with positive, supportive individuals who uplift and encourage you during difficult times. Seek out mentors, friends, or support groups who can provide guidance, perspective, and a listening ear.*

- **Practice self-care:** *Prioritize self-care to nourish your physical, emotional, and mental well-being. Engage in activities that bring you joy, relaxation, and rejuvenation. Set boundaries to protect your energy and time.*

- **Develop problem-solving skills:** *Enhance your problem-solving skills by breaking challenges down into smaller, manageable steps. Approach obstacles with a solution-oriented mindset, seeking creative and innovative approaches.*

- **Foster adaptability:** *Develop adaptability by embracing change and uncertainty. Cultivate flexibility and openness to new possibilities. Practice adjusting your plans and strategies when unexpected circumstances arise.*

- **Practice self-reflection:** *Engage in regular self-reflection to gain insights into your strengths, areas for growth, and patterns of behavior. Reflect on past experiences and identify the lessons learned from overcoming* *difficulties.*

» **Seek meaning and purpose:** *Connect with your values, passions, and purpose. Understanding your "why" provides a sense of meaning and fuels your resilience during challenging times.*

Navigating Setbacks and Building Resilience

» **Acceptance:** *Acknowledge and accept the reality of setbacks or failures. Allow yourself to experience the associated emotions, but avoid dwelling on them excessively. Understand that setbacks are part of the journey and offer opportunities for growth.*

» **Learn from failures:** *View failures as valuable lessons. Identify the insights, skills, or knowledge gained from each setback. Use these experiences as stepping stones for personal growth and improvement.*

» **Develop problem-solving skills:** *When faced with obstacles, break them down into smaller, manageable parts. Identify potential solutions and take proactive steps to overcome challenges. Seek assistance or guidance when needed.*

» **Cultivate optimism:** *Nurture an optimistic*

outlook by focusing on possibilities and positive outcomes. Practice gratitude for the lessons learned and the progress made, even in the face of setbacks.

» **Practice self-compassion:** *Treat yourself with kindness and compassion during difficult times. Recognize that setbacks are a natural part of life, and offer yourself understanding and support.*

» **Seek support:** *Reach out to trusted friends, family members, or professionals who can provide guidance, encouragement, and perspective. Share your challenges and allow others to offer their support and insights.*

» **Maintain perspective:** *During setbacks, it's easy to lose sight of the bigger picture. Remind yourself of your goals, aspirations, and the progress you have made. Stay focused on your long-term vision and keep moving forward.*

Remember, developing resilience is a journey, and it requires consistent practice and effort. Embrace setbacks as opportunities for growth, learn from them, and keep cultivating your resilience. By bouncing back from setbacks, you build inner strength, character, and a mindset that can overcome any obstacle on your path to unleashing your inner potential.

In the next section, we will explore the importance of setting purposeful goals and creating an action plan to bring our dreams and aspirations into reality.

Quiz Questions for Section IV.A: Developing Resilience: Bouncing Back from Setbacks

81. What is the main focus of Section IV.A?
82. Define resilience and explain its importance in personal growth and overcoming challenges.
83. **True or False**: Resilience is an innate trait that some people are born with, while others are not.
84. List three key components or skills involved in developing resilience.
85. How can reframing setbacks as opportunities for growth contribute to resilience?
86. Discuss the role of self-belief in building resilience.
87. Explain the concept of adaptive coping strategies and their significance in resilience.
88. **True or False**: Building resilience means avoiding or suppressing negative emotions.
89. What are some ways to cultivate a resilient mindset in the face of adversity?
90. How does developing resilience contribute to long-term success and well-being?

Exercises for Section IV.A: Developing Resilience: Bouncing Back from Setbacks

» **Reflection and Learning:** *Reflect on a recent setback or challenge you faced. Write down three lessons or insights you gained from the experience and how you can apply them to future situations.*

» **Growth Mindset Affirmations:** *Create a list of affirmations that promote a growth mindset and resilience. Repeat these affirmations daily to reinforce positive beliefs about your ability to bounce back from setbacks.*

» **Obstacle Course:** *Set up a physical or mental obstacle course that challenges your resilience. Design various stations or tasks that test your problem-solving skills, adaptability, and persistence. Complete the course and celebrate your achievements.*

» **Resilience Role Models:** *Identify individuals who embody resilience and have overcome significant setbacks. Research their stories and write a short essay or create a presentation highlighting their journey. Reflect on the lessons you can learn from their experiences.*

- » **Visualization and Resilience:** *Close your eyes and visualize yourself successfully navigating a challenging situation. Imagine feeling resilient, focused, and determined. Engage all your senses to make the visualization vivid and inspiring.*

- » **Resilience Journaling:** *Start a resilience journal to document your experiences, setbacks, and how you navigate through them. Write about your emotions, coping strategies, and the lessons you learn along the way. Use this journal as a tool for reflection and growth.*

- » **Resilience Circle:** *Gather a group of friends or family members and form a resilience circle. Share personal stories of resilience and setbacks, provide support, and offer constructive feedback and encouragement to one another.*

- » **Strengths Inventory:** *Identify and reflect on your strengths, skills, and resources that contribute to your resilience. Make a list of these assets and explore how you can leverage them during challenging times.*

- » **Resilience Visualization Board:** *Create a visualization board using images, quotes, and affirmations that represent resilience and overcoming setbacks. Display the board in a* *prominent place as a visual reminder of your resilience journey.*

» **Resilience in Action:** *Identify a small challenge or task that you have been avoiding due to fear of failure or setbacks. Take action and face that challenge head-on. Embrace the opportunity to practice resilience and observe your growth throughout the process.*

Quiz Answers for Section IV.A: Developing Resilience: Bouncing Back from Setbacks

81. The main focus of Section IV.A is developing resilience and the ability to bounce back from setbacks.
82. Resilience is the capacity to adapt, recover, and grow stronger in the face of adversity or challenges. It is important for personal growth as it promotes perseverance, problem-solving, and emotional well-being.
83. **False.** Resilience is a skill that can be developed and strengthened through practice and learning.
84. Three key components or skills involved in developing resilience are self-belief, adaptive coping strategies, and the ability to reframe setbacks as opportunities for growth.
85. Reframing setbacks as opportunities for growth allows individuals to shift their perspective and find meaning or valuable lessons in difficult situations, which contributes to resilience.
86. Self-belief plays a crucial role in building resilience as it fosters confidence, optimism, and the belief in one's ability to overcome challenges.
87. Adaptive coping strategies are healthy and effective ways of dealing with stress and adversity. They involve problem-solving, seeking support, and engaging in self-care

activities.

88. **False.** Building resilience does not mean avoiding or suppressing negative emotions. It means acknowledging and processing them in a healthy way while focusing on constructive actions and thoughts.
89. Cultivating a resilient mindset involves practicing self-compassion, maintaining a positive outlook, nurturing social connections, and embracing a growth mindset.
90. Developing resilience contributes to long-term success and well-being by enabling individuals to navigate challenges effectively, bounce back from setbacks, and maintain a positive and proactive attitude towards achieving their goals.

Setting Purposeful Goals and Creating an Action Plan

Goals provide direction, focus, and a sense of purpose in our lives. In this section, we will explore the importance of setting purposeful goals and creating an action plan to turn our aspirations into reality. By aligning our actions with our desires, we can make meaningful progress towards unleashing our inner potential and achieving lasting success.

The Power of Purposeful Goals

Setting purposeful goals allows us to clarify our vision, identify what truly matters to us, and create a roadmap for our personal growth and development. Goals provide a sense of direction and serve as a catalyst for action. They help us prioritize our time, energy, and resources towards activities that align with our aspirations.

» **Reflecting on Your Desires and Values:** *Begin by reflecting on your deepest desires and values. What do you truly want to achieve and experience in life? What aspects of your life are most important to you? By understanding your core values and aspirations, you can set goals that are aligned with your authentic self.*

» **Defining SMART Goals:** *SMART is an*

acronym that stands for Specific, Measurable, Achievable, Relevant, and Time-bound. When setting goals, ensure they are specific and clearly defined. Make them measurable, so you can track your progress and celebrate milestones. Ensure they are realistic and achievable within your current circumstances. Make them relevant to your overall vision and values. Lastly, set a timeframe or deadline to create a sense of urgency and accountability.

» **Long-Term and Short-Term Goals:** *Distinguish between long-term and short-term goals. Long-term goals represent the bigger picture and may span several years or even a lifetime. Short-term goals are smaller, actionable steps that contribute to the achievement of your long-term goals. Breaking down long-term goals into manageable short-term goals makes the journey more attainable and less overwhelming.*

Creating an Action Plan

An action plan is a structured roadmap that outlines the specific steps, resources, and timelines required to achieve your goals. It provides a clear path towards progress and keeps you focused and accountable. Here's a step-by-step guide to creating an effective action plan:

- » **Identify Specific Actions:** *Break down your goals into specific actions or tasks. Clearly define what needs to be done to move closer to your desired outcome. Each action should be actionable, measurable, and directly contribute to your goal.*

- » **Prioritize:** *Determine the order of importance for your actions. Identify which tasks require immediate attention and which can be addressed later. Prioritizing helps you allocate your time and resources effectively.*

- » **Set Deadlines:** *Assign deadlines to each action step. Having clear timelines creates a sense of urgency and motivates you to take consistent action. Be realistic in setting deadlines, considering other commitments and potential challenges.*

- » **Seek Support:** *Identify the resources, knowledge, or skills you need to accomplish your goals. Seek support from mentors, coaches, or experts in the field. Surround yourself with individuals who can provide guidance, advice, and encouragement.*

- » **Track Your Progress:** *Regularly monitor and evaluate your progress. Keep a journal or use a tracking system to record your actions and milestones. Tracking allows you to celebrate achievements, identify* *areas for improvement, and make necessary adjustments to your action plan.*

» **Stay Flexible and Adapt:** *Life is unpredictable, and circumstances may change along the way. Be open to adjusting your action plan as needed. Embrace flexibility and adaptability to overcome obstacles and stay on course.*

Overcoming Procrastination and Building Healthy Habits

Procrastination is a common challenge when working towards our goals. Here are strategies to overcome procrastination and develop healthy habits:

» **Break Tasks into Smaller Steps:** *Large tasks can feel overwhelming and lead to procrastination. Break them down into smaller, more manageable steps. Focus on one step at a time, building momentum as you progress.*

» **Use Time Management Techniques:** *Implement time management techniques such as the Pomodoro Technique, where you work for a set amount of time (e.g., 25 minutes) followed by a short break. This approach helps increase focus and productivity.*

- **Create a Supportive Environment:** *Design an environment that minimizes distractions and supports your productivity. Remove temptations, create a designated workspace, and surround yourself with motivational cues or affirmations.*

- **Cultivate Self-Discipline:** *Develop self-discipline by practicing consistency and commitment to your goals. Build routines and rituals that reinforce positive habits and reinforce your progress.*

- **Celebrate Milestones:** *Celebrate your achievements and milestones along the way. Acknowledging your progress boosts motivation and reinforces positive behaviors.*

Remember, setting purposeful goals and creating an action plan is a dynamic process. Regularly review and adjust your goals and action steps as you progress and gain new insights. Stay committed to the journey and remain open to learning and growth.

In the next section, we will explore overcoming procrastination and creating healthy habits to support our personal and professional development.

Quiz Questions for Section IV.B: Setting Purposeful Goals and Creating an Action Plan

91. What is the main focus of Section IV.B?
92. Define the concept of a growth mindset and explain its relevance to setting purposeful goals.
93. **True or False**: Goal setting should only be focused on long-term objectives.
94. List three benefits of setting purposeful goals.
95. How can the SMART goal-setting framework help in creating effective action plans?
96. Discuss the importance of breaking down long-term goals into smaller, manageable steps.
97. What are some strategies for staying motivated and committed to achieving goals?
98. **True or False**: Flexibility and adaptability are essential when it comes to goal setting.
99. Explain the concept of accountability and its role in goal achievement.
100. How can celebrating milestones and progress contribute to sustaining motivation and progress?

Exercises for Section IV.B: Setting Purposeful Goals and Creating an Action Plan

» **Goal Reflection:** *Reflect on your long-term goals and write a paragraph describing why each goal is important to you. Visualize the outcomes and benefits of achieving those goals.*

» **Vision Board:** *Create a vision board that represents your long-term goals. Use images, words, and symbols that resonate with your aspirations. Display the vision board in a visible place as a daily reminder of your objectives.*

» **Goal Mapping:** *Create a visual roadmap of your goals by drawing a flowchart or using a mind-mapping tool. Connect your long-term goals to intermediate and short-term goals, and identify the actions required to achieve each milestone.*

» **Action Plan Tracker:** *Develop an action plan tracker to monitor your progress toward your goals. Break down your goals into specific tasks or action steps and track your completion of each task. Celebrate each milestone achieved.*

- » **Goal Buddy System:** *Partner with a friend or accountability buddy who shares similar goals. Regularly meet or check in with each other to discuss progress, challenges, and provide support and encouragement.*

- » **Time Blocking:** *Use time-blocking techniques to allocate specific time slots in your schedule dedicated to working on your goals. Prioritize these blocks of time and treat them as non-negotiable appointments with yourself.*

- » **Positive Affirmations:** *Develop a set of positive affirmations related to your goals. Repeat these affirmations daily to reinforce your belief in your ability to achieve your goals and overcome any obstacles.*

- » **Reverse Engineering:** *Start with your long-term goal and work backward to identify the necessary steps required to achieve it. Break down the steps into smaller, manageable actions and create a timeline for completion.*

- » **Visualization and Goal Achievement:** *Practice visualization exercises where you vividly imagine yourself accomplishing your goals. Engage your senses and emotions, and experience the joy and satisfaction of achieving what you desire.*

» **Gratitude Journaling:** *Keep a gratitude journal to reflect on the progress you've made toward your goals. Write down three things you are grateful for each day, focusing on the positive aspects of your journey and the steps you've taken.*

Quiz Answers for Section IV.B: Setting Purposeful Goals and Creating an Action Plan

91. The main focus of Section IV.B is setting purposeful goals and creating an action plan to achieve them.

92. A growth mindset is the belief that abilities and intelligence can be developed through dedication and hard work. It is relevant to goal setting as it fosters a belief in one's capacity to learn, improve, and overcome obstacles.

93. **False.** Goal setting should encompass both long-term and short-term objectives to provide direction and motivation.

94. Three benefits of setting purposeful goals include clarity and focus, increased motivation, and a sense of achievement and progress.

95. The SMART goal-setting framework stands for Specific, Measurable, Achievable, Relevant, and Time-bound. It helps ensure that goals are clear, well-defined, and have a specific timeline, increasing the likelihood of successful implementation.

96. Breaking down long-term goals into smaller steps makes them more manageable and allows for a sense of progress and achievement along the way.

97. Strategies for staying motivated and committed to goals include tracking progress, seeking support and accountability, visualizing success, and celebrating milestones.

98. **True.** Flexibility and adaptability are crucial because circumstances and priorities may change, requiring adjustments to goals and action plans.
99. Accountability refers to taking responsibility for one's actions and progress toward goals. It involves creating systems or seeking external support to ensure commitment and follow-through.
100. Celebrating milestones and progress provides a sense of accomplishment, boosts motivation, and reinforces positive behaviors, making it more likely to sustain effort and progress.

Overcoming Procrastination and Creating Healthy Habits

Procrastination is a common challenge that can hinder our progress and prevent us from unleashing our inner potential. In this section, we will explore the causes of procrastination and provide strategies to overcome it. Additionally, we will discuss the importance of creating healthy habits that support our personal and professional growth.

Understanding Procrastination

Procrastination is the act of delaying or avoiding tasks that require our attention and effort. It often stems from a combination of factors, including fear of failure, lack of motivation, perfectionism, overwhelm, and a desire for immediate gratification. By understanding the underlying causes of procrastination, we can develop effective strategies to overcome it.

» **Identify the Root Causes:** *Reflect on the reasons behind your procrastination. Is it fear of failure or success? Are you overwhelmed by the task at hand? Are you lacking clarity or motivation? Identifying the root causes will help you address them directly.*

» **Fear of Failure:** *The fear of failure can paralyze us and prevent us from taking* *action. Shift your perspective and embrace failure as an opportunity for growth and learning. Understand that setbacks are a natural part of the journey towards success.*

- » **Perfectionism:** *Perfectionism often leads to procrastination as we wait for the perfect conditions or the perfect outcome. Embrace a mindset of progress over perfection. Recognize that taking imperfect action is better than no action at all.*

- » **Break Tasks into Smaller Steps:** *Large tasks can be overwhelming and contribute to procrastination. Break them down into smaller, manageable steps. Focus on completing one step at a time, building momentum as you go.*

- » **Set Realistic Goals and Deadlines:** *Set realistic goals and establish deadlines for yourself. Ensure that your goals are attainable and align with your overall vision. Setting deadlines creates a sense of urgency and helps prioritize your tasks.*

- » **Create a Productive Environment:** *Design an environment that fosters productivity and minimizes distractions. Remove potential distractions such as social media notifications or unnecessary clutter. Create a dedicated workspace that promotes* *focus and concentration.*

» **Practice Time Management:** *Implement effective time management techniques, such as creating a schedule, prioritizing tasks, and allocating specific time slots for focused work. Use tools like timers or productivity apps to stay on track.*

» **Find Your Motivation:** *Understand what motivates you and use it as a driving force. Whether it's visualizing your desired outcome, rewarding yourself for completing tasks, or seeking accountability from a mentor or friend, find strategies that keep you motivated and engaged.*

Creating Healthy Habits

In addition to overcoming procrastination, cultivating healthy habits is crucial for long-term success and personal growth. Habits are the building blocks of our daily lives, and by consciously shaping them, we can create positive and productive routines.

» **Start Small:** *Begin by focusing on one habit at a time. Start with a small, achievable change that you can incorporate into your daily routine. Once that habit becomes ingrained, move on to the next one.*

» **Set Clear Intentions:** *Clearly define the habit you want to develop and the purpose* *behind it. Understanding why the habit is important to you will help you stay committed and motivated.*

» **Consistency is Key:** *Consistency is crucial when forming habits. Aim to perform the habit consistently, preferably daily, to reinforce the behavior and make it a natural part of your routine.*

» **Visual Reminders:** *Use visual cues or reminders to reinforce the habit. Place sticky notes, visual representations, or affirmations in visible areas as a constant reminder of your intention.*

» **Accountability and Support:** *Share your habit-building journey with an accountability partner or join a supportive community. Having someone to share your progress, challenges, and successes with can provide motivation and encouragement.*

» **Track Your Progress:** *Keep track of your habit-building efforts. Use a habit tracker or journal to monitor your consistency and reflect on your progress. Celebrate milestones and use any setbacks as learning opportunities.*

» **Practice Self-Compassion:** *Be kind to yourself during the habit-building process.*

Understand that setbacks and slip-ups are normal. Instead of berating yourself, approach them with self-compassion and a focus on learning and growth.

» **Continual Evaluation and Adjustment:** *Regularly evaluate your habits and their impact on your life. Adjust them as needed to ensure they align with your goals and values. As you grow and evolve, your habits may need to evolve as well.*

By overcoming procrastination and cultivating healthy habits, you will create a solid foundation for sustained personal and professional growth. Remember, it's the consistent daily actions that lead to significant long-term results. Embrace the process, be patient with yourself, and keep your focus on the positive changes you are making.

In the next section, we will explore the importance of nurturing relationships and support systems in our journey of personal growth and success.

Quiz Questions for Section IV.C: Overcoming Procrastination and Creating Healthy Habits

101. What is the main focus of Section IV.C?
102. Define procrastination and explain why it can hinder personal growth.
103. **True or False**: Procrastination is always a result of laziness.
104. What are some common underlying causes of procrastination?
105. Name three strategies for overcoming procrastination.
106. How can breaking tasks into smaller, manageable parts help in combating procrastination?
107. **True or False**: Creating a routine and establishing healthy habits can help in reducing procrastination.
108. Discuss the importance of self-awareness in addressing and overcoming procrastination.
109. How does accountability play a role in overcoming procrastination?
110. What are some techniques for cultivating healthy habits that support productivity and goal achievement?

Exercises for Section IV.C: Overcoming Procrastination and Creating Healthy Habits

» **Procrastination Diary:** *Keep a diary where you track instances of procrastination. Write down the tasks you delayed and reflect on the reasons behind your procrastination. Use this awareness to develop strategies to overcome it.*

» **Time Management Matrix:** *Create a time management matrix with four quadrants: Urgent and Important, Important but Not Urgent, Urgent but Not Important, Not Urgent and Not Important. Prioritize your tasks and identify which activities contribute to your long-term goals.*

» **Pomodoro Technique:** *Try the Pomodoro Technique for time management. Set a timer for 25 minutes and focus on a specific task without interruptions. Take a short break, then repeat. Track your productivity and notice the impact on your ability to tackle tasks.*

» **Habit Stacking:** *Choose an existing habit and stack a new habit you want to develop onto it. For example, if you want to start reading more, make it a habit to read for 10* *minutes before bedtime.*

» **Implementation Intentions:** *Write down specific implementation intentions for tasks you tend to procrastinate on. For example, "When I finish breakfast, I will start working on my most important task for 30 minutes."*

» **Procrastination Reflection:** *Reflect on the underlying reasons for your procrastination. Write a journal entry exploring any fears, perfectionism, or self-doubt that may contribute to your procrastination habits. Challenge these beliefs and develop positive affirmations.*

» **Habit Tracker:** *Create a habit tracker to monitor your progress in developing healthy habits. Track activities such as exercise, meditation, or reading daily. Celebrate streaks and milestones to reinforce the importance of consistency.*

» **Environment Optimization:** *Evaluate your physical and digital environment for potential distractions. Create a clutter-free workspace, remove unnecessary notifications from your phone, and design an environment that supports focus and productivity.*

» **Reward System:** *Set up a reward system for accomplishing tasks and sticking to* *your habits. Establish meaningful rewards for yourself, such as treating yourself to a favorite activity or item, upon completing important milestones.*

» **Visualization and Future Self:** *Practice visualization exercises where you imagine your future self who has overcome procrastination and has developed healthy habits. Visualize the positive impact it has on your life, productivity, and overall well-being.*

Quiz Answers for Section IV.C: Overcoming Procrastination and Creating Healthy Habits

101. The main focus of Section IV.C is overcoming procrastination and creating healthy habits.

102. Procrastination is the act of delaying or postponing tasks or actions. It hinders personal growth because it can lead to missed opportunities, increased stress, and reduced productivity.

103. **False.** Procrastination can stem from various factors, including fear, perfectionism, overwhelm, or a lack of clarity.

104. Some common underlying causes of procrastination include fear of failure, lack of motivation or interest, perfectionism, feeling overwhelmed, and poor time management skills.

105. Strategies for overcoming procrastination include breaking tasks into smaller parts, setting deadlines, using time management techniques, eliminating distractions, building accountability, practicing self-discipline, and developing a positive mindset.

106. Breaking tasks into smaller, manageable parts helps in combating procrastination by making tasks feel less overwhelming and more achievable. It increases motivation and provides a sense of progress as each smaller part is completed.

107. **True.** Creating a routine and establishing

healthy habits can help reduce procrastination by providing structure, promoting discipline, and creating a positive work environment that supports productivity.

108. Self-awareness is important in addressing and overcoming procrastination because it helps identify underlying triggers, patterns, and thought processes that contribute to procrastination. It allows for targeted strategies and interventions.

109. Accountability plays a role in overcoming procrastination by providing external support and motivation. It involves sharing goals and progress with others, seeking an accountability partner, or using tools and apps that track and monitor productivity.

110. Techniques for cultivating healthy habits that support productivity and goal achievement include habit stacking, creating implementation intentions, optimizing your environment, using rewards and incentives, and visualizing your future self.

V. Nurturing Relationships and Support Systems

Cultivating Empathy and Effective Communication

In our journey of personal growth and unleashing our inner potential, nurturing relationships and developing effective communication skills play a vital role. In this section, we will explore the power of empathy and how it enhances our connections with others. We will also delve into the art of effective communication, which allows us to express ourselves authentically and build harmonious relationships.

Understanding Empathy

Empathy is the ability to understand and share the feelings of another person. It is a fundamental aspect of human connection and plays a significant role in building strong, meaningful relationships. By cultivating empathy, we develop a deeper understanding of others, foster compassion, and create an environment of trust and support.

» **Active Listening:** *Active listening is an essential component of empathy. Practice giving your full attention to others when they speak, without interrupting or formulating responses in your mind. Maintain eye contact, nod, and use verbal cues to show that you are engaged in the conversation.*

» **Perspective-Taking:** *Put yourself in*

the shoes of others and try to see things from their perspective. This helps you gain insight into their emotions, experiences, and challenges. It allows you to respond with greater understanding and compassion.

» **Non-Judgmental Attitude:** *Approach interactions with a non-judgmental mindset. Suspend your preconceived notions and biases, and strive to see individuals as they are, without labeling or categorizing them. This creates a safe space for open and honest communication.*

» **Emotional Awareness:** *Develop your emotional awareness by understanding and recognizing your own emotions. This self-awareness enables you to better empathize with others, as you can relate to their emotional experiences.*

» **Validate Emotions:** *Validating someone's emotions means acknowledging and accepting their feelings without judgment. Show empathy by saying phrases such as, "I understand how you feel," or "It's okay to feel that way." This validation helps individuals feel heard and understood.*

» **Practice Empathetic Responses:** *Respond to others with empathy by reflecting their feelings and experiences. Use phrases like,*

"It sounds like you're feeling..." or "I can imagine that must have been difficult for you." These responses show that you are actively engaging in understanding their emotions.

» **Cultivate Curiosity:** *Curiosity about others fosters empathy. Ask open-ended questions to encourage individuals to share their thoughts and feelings. Be genuinely interested in their responses and seek to learn from their experiences.*

» **Show Empathy through Body Language:** *Non-verbal cues also convey empathy. Maintain an open and welcoming body posture, use facial expressions that reflect understanding and concern, and provide comforting gestures when appropriate.*

Effective Communication

In addition to empathy, effective communication is essential for building healthy and fulfilling relationships. Effective communication allows us to express ourselves clearly, listen actively, and resolve conflicts with respect and understanding. Here are key strategies to enhance your communication skills:

» **Clear and Concise Expression:** *Communicate your thoughts and feelings in a clear and concise manner. Use simple* *language, avoid jargon, and be mindful of the tone and delivery of your message. Clarity promotes understanding and minimizes misunderstandings.*

» **Active Listening:** *Actively listen to others when they speak. Give them your full attention, maintain eye contact, and be present in the moment. Avoid interrupting and allow individuals to express themselves fully before responding.*

» **Non-Verbal Communication:** *Pay attention to non-verbal cues such as body language, facial expressions, and tone of voice. Be aware of your own non-verbal communication and ensure that it aligns with your intended message. Non-verbal cues often convey more meaning than words alone.*

» **Empathetic Communication:** *Incorporate empathy into your communication. Show understanding, validate emotions, and respond with compassion. Acknowledge the other person's perspective and express empathy in your verbal and non-verbal responses.*

» **Open and Honest Expression:** *Foster an environment of open and honest communication. Encourage individuals to* *express their thoughts and feelings without fear of judgment or reprisal. Create a safe space where everyone's voice is valued and respected.*

» **Conflict Resolution:** *Develop skills in resolving conflicts effectively and constructively. Practice active listening, seek to understand all perspectives, and aim for win-win solutions. Use "I" statements to express your feelings and needs without blaming or criticizing others.*

» **Mindful Communication:** *Cultivate mindfulness in your communication. Be present, listen attentively, and respond thoughtfully. Avoid distractions and give your full focus to the conversation at hand. Mindful communication fosters deeper connections and understanding.*

» **Feedback and Appreciation:** *Provide constructive feedback when necessary, focusing on specific behaviors or actions rather than personal attacks. Balance feedback with appreciation and acknowledgment of strengths. Celebrate achievements and express gratitude for the contributions of others.*

By cultivating empathy and developing effective communication skills, you create a nurturing environment for building and maintaining healthy relationships. These skills not only enhance your personal connections but also contribute to your overall success and fulfillment in life.

In the next section, we will explore the importance of building healthy boundaries and relationships, empowering you to create meaningful connections while safeguarding your well-being and personal growth.

Quiz Questions for Section V.A: Cultivating Empathy and Effective Communication

111. What is the main focus of Section V.A?
112. Define empathy and explain its importance in nurturing relationships.
113. **True or False**: Empathy is solely about understanding others' emotions.
114. Name three techniques for cultivating empathy.
115. How does active listening contribute to effective communication?
116. Discuss the role of nonverbal communication in building empathy.
117. **True or False**: Empathy requires you to agree with others' perspectives.
118. How can empathy enhance your relationships and support systems?
119. What are some potential barriers to empathy, and how can they be overcome?
120. How does practicing empathy benefit your personal growth and well-being?

Exercises for Section V.A: Cultivating Empathy and Effective Communication

» **Empathy Journal:** *Keep a journal where you reflect on your interactions with others and identify moments where you demonstrated empathy or missed opportunities to be empathetic. Write down ways you can improve your empathy skills in future interactions.*

» **Perspective-Taking Exercise:** *Choose a person in your life and imagine yourself in their shoes. Write a letter or journal entry from their perspective, expressing their thoughts, feelings, and challenges. This exercise helps develop empathy by fostering a deeper understanding of others' experiences.*

» **Empathy Interviews:** *Conduct empathy interviews with friends, family members, or colleagues. Ask open-ended questions and actively listen to their responses. Practice reflecting their emotions and experiences back to them, showing genuine empathy and understanding.*

» **Emotional Mirror:** *Find a partner and sit facing each other. Take turns expressing different emotions non-verbally through facial expressions, gestures, and* *body language. Practice mirroring each other's emotions to develop empathy and attunement.*

- » **Empathy Circle:** *Gather a small group of friends or family members for an empathy circle. Each person takes turns sharing their experiences, while others actively listen without judgment. The goal is to create a safe space for empathy and understanding.*

- » **Storytelling Exchange:** *Share personal stories with a partner or in a group setting. Listen attentively to each other's stories and identify common emotions and themes. This exercise builds empathy by connecting through shared experiences.*

- » **Media Analysis:** *Choose a movie, TV show, or book that explores diverse perspectives or portrays complex emotions. Analyze the characters' motivations, challenges, and emotions. Discuss the empathy you felt towards different characters and reflect on how it relates to real-life situations.*

- » **Random Acts of Kindness:** *Engage in acts of kindness and compassion towards strangers or acquaintances. Offer help, give compliments, or engage in small gestures that demonstrate empathy and care for others.*

- **Empathy Building Games:** *Play empathy-building games or activities such as "Two Truths and a Lie," where participants share personal experiences and others guess the lie. This fosters understanding and empathy by encouraging active listening and curiosity.*

- **Conflict Resolution Practice:** *Role-play conflict scenarios with a partner or group. Practice active listening, expressing emotions constructively, and finding common ground. This exercise enhances empathy and communication skills in challenging situations.*

Quiz Answers for Section V.A: Cultivating Empathy and Effective Communication

111. The main focus of Section V.A is cultivating empathy and effective communication.

112. Empathy is the ability to understand and share the feelings of others. It is important in nurturing relationships because it fosters connection, trust, and mutual understanding.

113. **False.** Empathy involves not only understanding others' emotions but also showing compassion, validating their experiences, and offering support.

114. Techniques for cultivating empathy include active listening, perspective-taking, practicing nonjudgment, seeking to understand before being understood, and expressing empathy through words and actions.

115. Active listening contributes to effective communication by demonstrating respect, understanding, and genuine interest in what the other person is saying. It helps build trust and fosters a deeper connection.

116. Nonverbal communication, such as body language, facial expressions, and tone of voice, plays a crucial role in building empathy. It helps to understand and interpret others' emotions and feelings beyond their words.

117. **False.** Empathy does not require you to agree with others' perspectives. It is about acknowledging and validating their emotions

and experiences without necessarily endorsing their viewpoints.

118. Empathy enhances relationships and support systems by fostering trust, understanding, and connection. It promotes effective communication, conflict resolution, and mutual respect, leading to healthier and more fulfilling interactions.

119. Barriers to empathy can include biases, preconceived notions, lack of self-awareness, and emotional disconnect. They can be overcome through self-reflection, active listening, open-mindedness, and a willingness to challenge and expand one's perspective.

120. Practicing empathy benefits personal growth and well-being by fostering deeper connections, improving communication skills, promoting emotional intelligence, and enhancing overall empathy towards oneself and others.

Building Healthy Boundaries and Relationships

As we continue our journey of personal growth and unleashing our inner potential, it is crucial to understand the significance of building healthy boundaries and nurturing relationships. Boundaries act as guidelines that define how we interact with others, while healthy relationships provide support, encouragement, and opportunities for growth. In this section, we will explore the importance of establishing and maintaining healthy boundaries and delve into strategies for building and nurturing positive relationships.

Understanding Boundaries

Boundaries are essential for maintaining our well-being, protecting our values, and fostering healthy connections with others. They define what is acceptable and unacceptable in our relationships, and they help establish a sense of self-worth and self-respect. Here are key aspects to consider when building healthy boundaries:

» **Self-Awareness:** *Develop a deep understanding of your needs, values, and personal limits. Reflect on what feels comfortable and uncomfortable for you in different areas of your life, such as work, friendships, and romantic relationships. This self-awareness forms the foundation for* *establishing boundaries.*

- » **Assertiveness:** *Cultivate assertiveness, which allows you to communicate your boundaries confidently and respectfully. Practice expressing your needs and desires without fear of rejection or conflict. Remember, setting boundaries is a healthy act of self-care and self-respect.*

- » **Clear Communication:** *Clearly communicate your boundaries to others in a respectful manner. Use "I" statements to express your needs and expectations, and be specific about what behaviors or actions are acceptable or unacceptable. Effective communication is essential for others to understand and honor your boundaries.*

- » **Consistency:** *Consistency is key in maintaining boundaries. Ensure that your words and actions align with the boundaries you have set. People will learn to respect your boundaries when they see you consistently enforcing them.*

- » **Flexibility and Adaptability:** *While boundaries are important, it is also essential to be flexible and adaptable when appropriate. Consider the context and the needs of others, and be willing to adjust your boundaries within reasonable limits.*

Building Positive Relationships

Building and nurturing positive relationships is a crucial aspect of personal growth and unleashing our inner potential. Healthy relationships provide support, encouragement, and opportunities for growth. Here are strategies for cultivating positive connections:

» **Mutual Respect:** *Cultivate mutual respect in your relationships. Treat others with kindness, empathy, and understanding. Respect their boundaries, opinions, and values, just as you expect them to respect yours.*

» **Active Listening:** *Practice active listening to foster genuine connections. Give your full attention to the person you are communicating with, maintain eye contact, and listen with empathy. Seek to understand their perspectives and validate their feelings.*

» **Authenticity and Vulnerability:** *Be authentic and vulnerable in your relationships. Share your thoughts, feelings, and experiences honestly, and encourage others to do the same. Authenticity creates deeper connections and builds trust.*

» **Healthy Conflict Resolution:** *Conflict is a natural part of any relationship, but how we handle it determines the strength of the bond. Learn healthy conflict resolution skills, such* *as active listening, seeking understanding, and finding win-win solutions. Approach conflicts with respect and a willingness to find common ground.*

» **Support and Encouragement:** *Provide support and encouragement to the people in your life. Celebrate their successes, offer a lending hand in challenging times, and be a source of positivity and inspiration. Building others up contributes to a nurturing and empowering relationship.*

» **Boundaries in Relationships:** *Establish and respect boundaries within your relationships. Communicate openly about expectations, personal space, and individual needs. Encourage healthy boundaries in others and be mindful of crossing them.*

» **Growth Mindset in Relationships:** *Embrace a growth mindset within your relationships. Recognize that both you and others have the potential for growth and development. Encourage each other's goals and dreams, and provide support during challenges and setbacks.*

By actively building healthy boundaries and nurturing positive relationships, you create a supportive network that fuels your personal growth and unleashes your inner potential. These relationships become a source of strength, inspiration, and accountability as you continue your journey towards lasting success.

In the next section, we will explore the role of mentorship and accountability in our personal growth, discovering how these elements can significantly impact our path to success.

Quiz Questions for Section V.B: Building Healthy Boundaries and Relationships

121. What is the main focus of Section V.B?
122. Define boundaries and explain their significance in building healthy relationships.
123. **True or False**: Setting boundaries means being selfish or uncaring.
124. Name three signs that indicate you may have weak or unclear boundaries in a relationship.
125. How can effective communication contribute to building healthy boundaries?
126. Discuss the importance of self-awareness in establishing and maintaining boundaries.
127. **True or False**: Building healthy boundaries means cutting off all connections with others.
128. What are some strategies for asserting and reinforcing personal boundaries?
129. How does building healthy boundaries impact your overall well-being and self-esteem?
130. Why is it essential to regularly evaluate and adjust boundaries in relationships?

Exercises for Section V.B: Building Healthy Boundaries and Relationships

» **Boundary Setting Scenarios:** *Create various scenarios where you may encounter boundary challenges in relationships. Write down how you would assert and communicate your boundaries effectively in each situation.*

» **Boundary Visualization:** *Close your eyes and visualize yourself surrounded by a protective bubble. Imagine this bubble representing your personal boundaries. Visualize it growing stronger and impenetrable as you affirm your right to establish and maintain healthy boundaries.*

» **Boundary Audit:** *Take inventory of your current relationships and identify any instances where your boundaries may have been crossed. Reflect on why it happened and what steps you can take to reinforce those boundaries moving forward.*

» **Assertiveness Role-Play:** *Pair up with a friend or family member and practice assertive communication. Take turns asserting your boundaries in different scenarios, focusing on clarity, respect, and firmness.*

- » **Boundary-Setting Letter:** *Write a letter to someone who has repeatedly crossed your boundaries. Clearly express how their behavior has impacted you and state your boundaries going forward. This exercise can help you articulate your needs and reinforce your boundaries.*

- » **Relationship Boundaries Check-In:** *Schedule a check-in conversation with a close friend or partner to discuss and reassess your boundaries in the relationship. Share your expectations, listen to their needs, and find common ground for establishing healthier boundaries.*

- » **Boundary-Building Affirmations:** *Create a list of affirmations that reinforce your commitment to building healthy boundaries. Repeat them daily to strengthen your belief in your right to set and enforce boundaries.*

- » **Relationship Contract:** *Develop a relationship contract or agreement with someone important to you. Outline mutual boundaries, expectations, and commitments to ensure a healthy and respectful relationship. Regularly review and update the contract as needed.*

- » **Boundary Visualization Art:** *Use art materials to visually represent your* *boundaries. Draw or paint an image that symbolizes your personal boundaries and hang it in a visible place as a reminder of their importance.*

» **Boundary Support Group:** *Join or create a support group where individuals can share experiences and strategies related to building and maintaining healthy boundaries. This provides a space for validation, guidance, and accountability.*

Quiz Answers for Section V.B: Building Healthy Boundaries and Relationships

121. The main focus of Section V.B is building healthy boundaries and relationships.

122. Boundaries refer to personal limits and guidelines that define what is acceptable or unacceptable in relationships. They are significant in building healthy relationships because they establish respect, protect individual needs, and foster mutual understanding.

123. **False.** Setting boundaries is about self-care and ensuring that your needs are met. It is not selfish but necessary for maintaining healthy relationships.

124. Signs of weak or unclear boundaries in a relationship include feeling overwhelmed, resentful, or taken advantage of, having difficulty saying no, and experiencing a lack of personal space or privacy.

125. Effective communication contributes to building healthy boundaries by enabling clear expression of needs, expectations, and limits. It allows for open dialogue, understanding, and negotiation in relationships.

126. Self-awareness is crucial in establishing and maintaining boundaries as it helps you recognize your values, triggers, and personal limits. It allows you to communicate your boundaries effectively and make choices aligned with your well-being.

127. **False.** Building healthy boundaries does not mean cutting off all connections. It means creating a balance between personal needs and the needs of others while maintaining respect and self-care.

128. Strategies for asserting and reinforcing personal boundaries include clear communication, using "I" statements, saying no without guilt, practicing self-care, seeking support, and being consistent with boundary enforcement.

129. Building healthy boundaries positively impacts overall well-being and self-esteem. It promotes self-respect, reduces stress and resentment, enhances relationship satisfaction, and allows for healthy self-expression.

130. It is essential to regularly evaluate and adjust boundaries in relationships to accommodate personal growth, changing needs, and evolving dynamics. Regular assessment ensures that boundaries remain relevant, effective, and supportive in maintaining healthy relationships.

The Role of Mentorship and Accountability

As we embark on our journey of personal growth and unleash our inner potential, it is essential to recognize the significant impact that mentorship and accountability can have on our path to success. Mentorship provides guidance, wisdom, and support from experienced individuals who have walked similar paths, while accountability ensures that we stay committed to our goals and take consistent action. In this section, we will explore the role of mentorship and accountability in nurturing our personal growth and unlocking our true potential.

Understanding Mentorship

Mentorship is a powerful relationship that offers invaluable support and guidance on our journey of personal growth. A mentor is someone who possesses knowledge, experience, and wisdom in a particular area of interest or expertise. They serve as a trusted advisor, providing insights, sharing their experiences, and offering constructive feedback to help us navigate challenges and make informed decisions. Here are key aspects to consider when seeking and engaging in mentorship:

» **Clarifying Your Goals and Needs:** *Before seeking a mentor, take the time to clarify your goals, aspirations, and areas where you seek* *guidance. Understand the specific expertise or knowledge you are looking for in a mentor. This clarity will help you identify the right mentor who aligns with your needs.*

- » **Finding a Mentor:** *Look for potential mentors within your network, professional associations, or through online platforms. Seek individuals who have achieved success in the areas you are passionate about. Reach out to them respectfully, expressing your admiration for their work and explaining why you believe they would be a valuable mentor for you.*

- » **Building a Relationship:** *Once you have found a mentor, focus on building a genuine and mutually beneficial relationship. Establish open and honest communication, demonstrating your commitment to personal growth and your willingness to learn. Respect their time and expertise, and be proactive in seeking their guidance.*

- » **Seeking Guidance and Feedback:** *Actively seek guidance and feedback from your mentor. Share your challenges, goals, and aspirations, and be open to their insights and perspectives. Be receptive to constructive criticism and use it as an opportunity for growth.*

- » **Learning from Their Experiences:** *Learn from your mentor's experiences and wisdom. Ask about their journey, the lessons they have learned, and the strategies they have used to overcome obstacles. Apply these insights to your own life and adapt them to your unique circumstances.*

- » **Cultivating a Growth Mindset:** *Embrace a growth mindset in your mentorship relationship. View challenges as opportunities for growth, and approach feedback and constructive criticism with a willingness to learn and improve. Foster a mindset that values continuous learning and development.*

Accountability for Personal Growth

Accountability plays a vital role in ensuring that we stay committed to our goals and take consistent action towards our personal growth. When we are accountable, we take responsibility for our choices, actions, and outcomes. Here are strategies for cultivating accountability:

- » **Set Clear Goals:** *Start by setting clear, specific, and measurable goals for your personal growth journey. Define what success means to you and outline the steps required to achieve your goals. Ensure your goals are realistic, challenging, and aligned with your* *values.*

» **Share Your Goals:** *Share your goals with trusted individuals who can provide support and hold you accountable. This can be a mentor, friend, family member, or an accountability partner. By vocalizing your goals, you create a sense of external motivation and increase your commitment to following through.*

» **Regular Progress Check-Ins:** *Schedule regular check-ins to evaluate your progress. Reflect on the actions you have taken, the obstacles you have encountered, and the lessons you have learned. Celebrate your achievements and adjust your strategies as needed to stay on track.*

» **Accountability Partnerships:** *Consider forming an accountability partnership with a like-minded individual who is also committed to personal growth. This partnership involves regularly sharing your goals, progress, and challenges with each other. Hold each other accountable by providing support, encouragement, and constructive feedback.*

» **Track Your Progress:** *Keep a record of your progress to visually track your journey. This can be done through a journal, a digital tracker, or a vision board. Seeing your* *progress visually reinforces your commitment and motivates you to keep moving forward.*

» **Reflect and Learn from Setbacks:** *Accept that setbacks and failures are part of the growth process. When faced with obstacles, view them as opportunities for learning and improvement. Reflect on the lessons you have learned, make adjustments, and continue to move forward with renewed determination.*

By embracing the power of mentorship and accountability, we create a strong support system that fuels our personal growth and enables us to unlock our true potential. A mentor provides guidance, wisdom, and valuable insights, while accountability ensures that we remain committed to our goals and take consistent action. Together, these elements propel us forward on our journey to lasting success.

In the next section, we will explore the importance of cultivating empathy and effective communication in nurturing our relationships and support systems. These skills are essential for building meaningful connections and fostering a supportive network that sustains our personal growth.

Quiz Questions for Section V.C: The Role of Mentorship and Accountability

131. What is the main focus of Section V.C?
132. Define mentorship and explain its importance in personal growth.
133. **True or False**: A mentor must always be someone older or more experienced than you.
134. Name three potential benefits of having a mentor in your life.
135. How can accountability partnerships or groups support your personal growth journey?
136. Discuss the difference between a mentor and a coach.
137. **True or False**: Mentorship is a one-way relationship where only the mentee receives guidance.
138. What are some ways to find a suitable mentor or accountability partner?
139. How can mentorship and accountability contribute to overcoming procrastination and developing healthy habits?
140. Why is it important to be an active and engaged mentee or accountability partner?

Exercises for Section V.C: The Role of Mentorship and Accountability

- **Mentorship Vision Board:** *Create a vision board that represents your ideal mentor or accountability partner. Include qualities, characteristics, and values you seek in a mentor. Display it in a visible place as a reminder of your aspirations.*

- **Mentorship Match Game:** *Create a deck of cards with mentorship-related qualities, such as wisdom, empathy, and experience. Play a matching game by flipping two cards at a time and explaining how those qualities contribute to an effective mentor-mentee relationship.*

- **Mentorship Reflection Journal:** *Start a journal where you reflect on your mentorship experiences. Write about lessons learned, insights gained, and the impact of mentorship on your personal growth. Make it a habit to write regularly.*

- **Accountability Partner Check-In:** *Schedule regular check-ins with your accountability partner. Use this time to review goals, progress, and challenges. Offer support and constructive feedback to each* *other to foster growth and accountability.*

» **Reverse Mentorship Exercise:** *Find an opportunity to share your knowledge or skills with someone who can benefit from your expertise. By becoming a mentor, you can gain a different perspective and enhance your leadership abilities.*

» **Mentorship Networking Event:** *Organize or participate in a mentorship networking event where individuals seeking mentors and potential mentors can connect and share insights. Foster a supportive and collaborative environment.*

» **Accountability Habit Tracker:** *Create a habit tracker that allows you and your accountability partner to track progress on specific goals or habits. Use visuals, colors, or stickers to make it engaging and rewarding.*

» **Virtual Mentorship Panel Discussion:** *Organize a virtual panel discussion with experienced mentors from different fields. Invite participants to ask questions and gain insights into various aspects of mentorship.*

» **Mentorship Appreciation Letter:** *Write a heartfelt appreciation letter to a mentor or accountability partner who has positively impacted your personal growth. Express* *gratitude and acknowledge their support and guidance.*

» **Accountability Game:** *Create a fun and interactive accountability game where you and your accountability partner compete or collaborate to achieve specific goals. Use rewards or incentives to make it engaging and enjoyable.*

Quiz Answers for Section V.C: The Role of Mentorship and Accountability

131. The main focus of Section V.C is the role of mentorship and accountability in personal growth.
132. Mentorship is a relationship where a more experienced or knowledgeable person guides, supports, and shares insights with a mentee to facilitate personal and professional development.
133. **False.** A mentor can be someone older or more experienced, but they can also be a peer or even younger. The focus is on the guidance and wisdom they provide rather than their age or experience level.
134. Potential benefits of having a mentor include gaining knowledge and expertise, expanding your network, receiving guidance and support, and accelerating personal growth and development.
135. Accountability partnerships or groups provide support, encouragement, and a sense of responsibility to stay committed to personal goals. They offer a platform for sharing progress, challenges, and receiving feedback.
136. A mentor typically provides guidance and wisdom based on their own experiences, while a coach focuses on asking powerful questions and helping individuals discover their own answers and strategies.
137. **False.** Mentorship is a mutually beneficial

relationship where both the mentor and mentee can learn and grow. It involves a reciprocal exchange of insights, knowledge, and support.

138. Ways to find a suitable mentor or accountability partner include joining professional organizations, attending networking events, reaching out to potential mentors directly, and utilizing mentorship programs or platforms.

139. Mentorship and accountability provide a structure and support system to overcome procrastination by setting clear goals, maintaining focus, and offering guidance and motivation. They also promote healthy habits by fostering discipline, consistency, and self-reflection.

140. It is important to be an active and engaged mentee or accountability partner to make the most of the relationship. This involves being open to feedback, seeking guidance, setting goals, taking initiative, and showing appreciation for the support received.

VI. Sustaining Personal Growth

Self-Care and Mindfulness Practices

In our fast-paced and demanding world, taking care of ourselves often takes a backseat to our responsibilities and commitments. However, self-care is not a luxury; it is a fundamental aspect of nurturing our personal growth and well-being. In this section, we will explore the importance of self-care and mindfulness practices in sustaining our personal growth journey and unlocking our true potential.

Understanding Self-Care

Self-care encompasses a wide range of activities and practices that prioritize our physical, mental, and emotional well-being. It involves intentionally taking time for ourselves, nourishing our bodies, rejuvenating our minds, and nurturing our souls. Here are key aspects to consider when incorporating self-care into your life:

» **Prioritizing Your Needs:** *Recognize that self-care is not selfish but rather essential for your overall well-being. Prioritize your needs by making self-care a non-negotiable part of your routine. Create space in your schedule for activities that bring you joy, relaxation, and rejuvenation.*

» **Physical Self-Care:** *Take care of your physical health by engaging in activities that* *promote vitality and wellness. This includes regular exercise, nourishing your body with nutritious foods, getting sufficient sleep, and attending to your healthcare needs. Listen to your body's signals and give it the care it deserves.*

» **Emotional Self-Care:** *Acknowledge and honor your emotions. Engage in activities that support your emotional well-being, such as journaling, practicing gratitude, engaging in hobbies, and seeking support from trusted friends or professionals. Allow yourself to feel and process your emotions in a healthy and constructive manner.*

» **Mental Self-Care:** *Nurture your mind by engaging in activities that stimulate your intellect and promote mental well-being. This can include reading books, solving puzzles, learning new skills, engaging in creative endeavors, and engaging in stimulating conversations. Set boundaries with technology and create space for mental relaxation and reflection.*

» **Spiritual Self-Care:** *Explore and cultivate practices that nourish your soul and connect you with something greater than yourself. This can include meditation, prayer, mindfulness, spending time in nature,* *engaging in acts of kindness, or participating in spiritual or religious practices that resonate with you.*

» **Creating Rituals:** *Incorporate self-care rituals into your daily, weekly, and monthly routines. These rituals serve as anchors that remind you to prioritize self-care. It can be as simple as enjoying a cup of tea in the morning, taking a walk in nature, or setting aside dedicated time for self-reflection and introspection.*

The Power of Mindfulness

Mindfulness is the practice of being fully present and engaged in the present moment, without judgment. It involves cultivating a non-reactive awareness of our thoughts, emotions, sensations, and surroundings. Mindfulness allows us to observe our experiences with clarity and acceptance, enhancing our overall well-being. Here's how mindfulness can support our personal growth:

» **Cultivating Present-Moment Awareness:** *Mindfulness helps us break free from the autopilot mode of living and brings us into the present moment. By cultivating present-moment awareness, we develop a deeper connection with ourselves, others, and the world around us.*

- » **Managing Stress and Anxiety:** *Mindfulness practices, such as deep breathing exercises, body scans, and meditation, can help us manage stress and anxiety. By paying attention to our breath and bodily sensations, we anchor ourselves in the present moment, reducing the grip of anxious thoughts and worries.*

- » **Enhancing Self-Awareness:** *Mindfulness allows us to observe our thoughts, emotions, and patterns of behavior without judgment. This heightened self-awareness enables us to recognize and understand our triggers, habitual reactions, and limiting beliefs. With this awareness, we gain the power to make conscious choices and cultivate positive change.*

- » **Fostering Emotional Well-being:** *Mindfulness helps us develop a compassionate and non-judgmental relationship with our emotions. Rather than suppressing or avoiding them, we learn to acknowledge and accept our emotions as they arise. This self-compassion and emotional resilience enable us to respond to challenges with greater equanimity and kindness.*

- » **Cultivating Focus and Clarity:** *Regular mindfulness practice improves our ability to* *concentrate and stay focused. By training our attention, we enhance our cognitive skills, decision-making abilities, and overall mental clarity. This heightened focus allows us to engage more fully in our endeavors and make intentional choices aligned with our goals.*

Incorporating Self-Care and Mindfulness into Your Life

Integrating self-care and mindfulness practices into your life requires commitment, consistency, and a genuine desire to nurture your well-being. Here are some strategies to help you incorporate these practices into your daily routine:

» **Set Intentions:** *Begin each day by setting intentions for self-care and mindfulness. Clarify what practices you want to engage in and how they will support your personal growth. Write them down or say them aloud to reinforce your commitment.*

» **Start Small:** *Begin with small, manageable steps to avoid overwhelm. Choose one self-care practice and one mindfulness practice to focus on initially. As you build consistency and experience the benefits, you can gradually expand and diversify your practices.*

» **Create Rituals and Routines:** *Establish*

dedicated times for self-care and mindfulness in your daily routine. Designate specific spaces or create a cozy corner in your home where you can engage in these practices without distractions.

» **Find Accountability and Support:** *Engage in self-care and mindfulness practices with a friend, partner, or support group. Share your goals, progress, and challenges, and hold each other accountable. Having a sense of community and support can enhance motivation and help you stay committed.*

» **Be Flexible and Adaptive:** *Recognize that self-care and mindfulness practices may evolve and change over time. Be open to exploring different practices and adapt them to suit your needs and preferences. Trust your intuition and listen to what your mind, body, and soul are calling for in each moment.*

Remember, self-care and mindfulness are not one-time endeavors but ongoing practices that require continuous cultivation. By making them integral parts of your life, you nourish your inner self, sustain your personal growth journey, and unlock your true potential.

In the next section, we will explore the importance of celebrating progress and practicing self-compassion as we continue on our path of personal growth. These practices provide essential support and encouragement, enabling us to navigate challenges with resilience and maintain a positive mindset.

Quiz Questions for Section VI.A: Self-Care and Mindfulness Practices

141. What is the main focus of Section VI.A?
142. Define self-care and explain why it is important for personal growth.
143. **True or False**: Self-care is only about pampering yourself and indulging in leisure activities.
144. Name three examples of self-care practices that promote physical well-being.
145. How does self-care contribute to mental and emotional well-being?
146. Discuss the relationship between self-care and productivity.
147. **True or False**: Self-care is a selfish act that takes away time and energy from others.
148. What are some self-care practices that can be incorporated into a daily routine?
149. How can mindfulness practices enhance self-care?
150. Why is it important to personalize your self-care routine according to your own needs and preferences?

Exercises for Section VI.A: Self-Care and Mindfulness Practices

- **Self-Care Menu:** *Create a self-care menu with different activities that promote self-care across various dimensions, such as physical, emotional, and social. Refer to this menu when you need inspiration for self-care practices.*

- **Mindful Eating Exercise:** *Practice mindful eating by selecting one meal or snack each day to eat slowly and attentively. Pay attention to the flavors, textures, and sensations of the food, and notice how it affects your overall well-being.*

- **Gratitude Journal:** *Start a gratitude journal and write down three things you are grateful for each day. This practice can help shift your focus to the positive aspects of life and enhance your overall well-being.*

- **Digital Detox Challenge:** *Dedicate a day or weekend to a digital detox challenge. Disconnect from technology and engage in activities that promote relaxation, creativity, and face-to-face interactions.*

- **Self-Care Playlist:** *Create a playlist of your favorite uplifting and calming songs. Use this playlist as a tool for relaxation, self-*

reflection, and mood enhancement.

- **Nature Walk Meditation:** *Go for a walk in nature and practice mindfulness. Focus on the sights, sounds, and sensations around you, allowing yourself to be fully present in the moment.*

- **Self-Care Accountability Partner:** *Find an accountability partner who shares an interest in self-care. Set goals together and support each other in prioritizing self-care practices.*

- **Creative Expression:** *Engage in a creative activity such as painting, writing, dancing, or playing an instrument. Express yourself freely and use this as a form of self-care and self-expression.*

- **Mindful Breathing Exercise:** *Practice a mindful breathing exercise. Take deep breaths, focusing on the sensations of each inhale and exhale. This exercise can help reduce stress and promote relaxation.*

- **Self-Care Commitment Contract:** *Create a commitment contract with yourself, outlining specific self-care practices you will prioritize each week. Sign and display it as a reminder of your commitment to self-care.*

Quiz Answers for Section VI.A: Self-Care and Mindfulness Practices

141. The main focus of Section VI.A is self-care and mindfulness practices for sustaining personal growth.

142. Self-care refers to intentional actions and practices that promote physical, mental, and emotional well-being. It is important for personal growth as it helps replenish energy, reduce stress, and enhance overall resilience and productivity.

143. **False.** While pampering and leisure activities can be part of self-care, it also includes activities that support your well-being, such as setting boundaries, prioritizing rest, and engaging in activities that bring joy and fulfillment.

144. Examples of self-care practices that promote physical well-being include regular exercise, nutritious eating, and adequate sleep.

145. Self-care contributes to mental and emotional well-being by providing opportunities for relaxation, stress reduction, self-reflection, and nurturing positive emotions.

146. Self-care and productivity are closely linked. When you prioritize self-care, you replenish your energy, enhance focus, and reduce burnout, which ultimately improves your productivity and performance.

147. **False.** Self-care is not selfish. It is a necessary practice to ensure your own well-being, which

in turn enables you to show up fully for others and be of greater support to them.

148. Examples of self-care practices that can be incorporated into a daily routine include setting aside time for yourself, engaging in hobbies or activities you enjoy, practicing gratitude, and engaging in mindfulness exercises.

149. Mindfulness practices enhance self-care by promoting present-moment awareness, reducing stress, improving self-compassion, and fostering a greater connection with yourself and your needs.

150. Personalizing your self-care routine is important because everyone's needs and preferences are unique. It allows you to tailor your self-care practices to what resonates with you and brings you the most benefit.

Celebrating Progress and Practicing Self-Compassion

In our journey of personal growth and self-mastery, it's crucial to acknowledge and celebrate our progress along the way. Oftentimes, we are quick to focus on our shortcomings or the gap between where we are and where we want to be. However, by intentionally celebrating our achievements, big and small, we cultivate a positive mindset and nourish our self-esteem. In this section, we will explore the importance of celebrating progress and practicing self-compassion as essential components of sustaining personal growth and unlocking our true potential.

The Power of Celebrating Progress

Celebrating progress is about recognizing and honoring the steps we've taken and the milestones we've reached on our journey of personal growth. It serves several important purposes:

» **Motivation and Momentum:** *Celebrating progress provides motivation and fuels our momentum. When we acknowledge our achievements, we experience a sense of pride and accomplishment, which encourages us to keep moving forward. It reinforces the belief that our efforts are worthwhile and that we are capable of creating positive change in our lives.*

- » **Positive Reinforcement:** *By celebrating progress, we reinforce positive habits, behaviors, and mindset shifts that have contributed to our growth. This positive reinforcement strengthens neural pathways in our brain associated with these changes, making them more ingrained and sustainable over time.*

- » **Cultivating Gratitude and Positivity:** *Celebrating progress cultivates gratitude and positivity. It shifts our focus from what is lacking or unfinished to what we have achieved and what is going well in our lives. This shift in perspective enhances our overall well-being and helps us maintain a positive mindset.*

- » **Building Resilience:** *Celebrating progress builds resilience by reminding us of our ability to overcome challenges and setbacks. It serves as evidence of our capacity to adapt, learn, and grow. When we encounter obstacles or face difficulties, reflecting on past achievements can inspire us to persevere and find solutions.*

Practicing Self-Compassion

In addition to celebrating progress, practicing self-compassion is crucial for sustaining personal growth. Self-compassion involves treating ourselves with kindness, understanding, and acceptance, especially during challenging times. Here's why self-compassion is essential:

- **Cultivating Inner Nurturance:** *Self-compassion allows us to nurture ourselves emotionally and provide the care and support we need. It involves extending the same compassion, empathy, and understanding to ourselves that we would offer to a loved one. By being kind and gentle with ourselves, we create a safe and supportive inner environment for personal growth.*

- **Embracing Imperfection:** *Self-compassion helps us embrace our imperfections and accept ourselves as we are, without judgment or self-criticism. It acknowledges that making mistakes, experiencing setbacks, and facing obstacles are natural parts of the growth process. By embracing imperfection, we free ourselves from the pressure of unrealistic expectations and allow room for learning and growth.*

- **Managing Self-Criticism and Inner Dialogue:** *Practicing self-compassion helps us manage our inner critic and negative self-talk. It allows us to respond to self-critical thoughts and beliefs with kindness and understanding. By challenging self-judgment* *and replacing it with self-compassion, we cultivate a positive and supportive inner dialogue that fosters personal growth.*

» **Building Emotional Resilience:** *Self-compassion builds emotional resilience by providing us with a stable and nurturing foundation during difficult times. It acknowledges our pain, validates our emotions, and offers self-care and self-soothing practices to help us navigate challenges. By offering ourselves compassion, we develop the strength and courage to face adversity and continue growing.*

Incorporating Celebration and Self-Compassion into Your Journey

To incorporate celebration and self-compassion into your personal growth journey, consider the following practices:

» **Gratitude and Reflection:** *Set aside time regularly to reflect on your progress and express gratitude for your achievements. Create a gratitude journal or dedicate a space in your existing journal to jot down moments of growth and accomplishments. This practice will help you shift your focus to the positive aspects of your journey and foster a sense of appreciation.*

» **Milestone Celebrations:** *Identify milestones or significant achievements along your path of personal growth. When you reach these milestones, celebrate them in meaningful ways. Treat yourself to something you enjoy, gather with loved ones to share your progress, or engage in a special activity that symbolizes your accomplishment. These celebrations reinforce your commitment and provide a sense of fulfillment.*

» **Self-Compassionate Self-Talk:** *Pay attention to your inner dialogue and practice self-compassion when facing challenges or setbacks. Instead of berating yourself for perceived failures or shortcomings, offer yourself words of kindness and understanding. Treat yourself as you would treat a dear friend who is going through a similar situation.*

» **Self-Care Rituals:** *Engage in self-care practices that nourish your mind, body, and soul. Develop a self-care routine that includes activities you find pleasurable, relaxing, or rejuvenating. This may include taking bubble baths, practicing yoga, spending time in nature, reading inspirational books, or engaging in creative hobbies. These practices enhance your well-being and provide a foundation of self-compassion.*

» ***Seek Support and Accountability:*** *Share your journey with a trusted friend, mentor, or support group. Connect with individuals who understand the importance of celebrating progress and practicing self-compassion. Share your achievements, challenges, and self-compassion practices with them. They can offer support, encouragement, and accountability on your growth path.*

Remember, celebrating progress and practicing self-compassion are ongoing practices that require intentional effort and self-awareness. Embrace the journey of personal growth with kindness, patience, and a willingness to acknowledge and honor your progress along the way. In the next section, we will explore the importance of embracing a lifelong learning mindset as a key element of sustaining personal growth and unlocking your true potential.

Quiz Questions for Section VI.B: Celebrating Progress and Practicing Self-Compassion

151. What is the main focus of Section VI.B?
152. Why is it important to celebrate your progress on your personal growth journey?
153. **True or False**: Self-compassion means being self-critical and judgmental of your mistakes.
154. How can celebrating progress and practicing self-compassion contribute to sustaining personal growth?
155. Name three ways you can celebrate your progress and achievements, no matter how small.
156. What are the benefits of practicing self-compassion when facing setbacks or failures?
157. **True or False**: Self-compassion is a sign of weakness or self-indulgence.
158. How can self-compassion help you maintain motivation and resilience?
159. Discuss the role of gratitude in both celebrating progress and practicing self-compassion.
160. How can you integrate the practice of self-compassion into your daily life?

Exercises for Section VI.B: Celebrating Progress and Practicing Self-Compassion

» **Progress Reflection:** *Take time to reflect on your personal growth journey so far. Write down three specific achievements or progress you have made, and acknowledge the effort and dedication it took to reach them.*

» **Self-Compassion Letter:** *Write a heartfelt letter to yourself, expressing kindness, understanding, and encouragement. Acknowledge your strengths and areas of growth, and offer yourself words of compassion and support.*

» **Celebratory Ritual:** *Create a personal ritual to celebrate your achievements. It can be as simple as lighting a candle, playing uplifting music, or treating yourself to something you enjoy. Use this ritual to acknowledge and honor your progress.*

» **Visualization Exercise:** *Close your eyes and visualize yourself accomplishing a future goal or overcoming a challenge. Embrace the feeling of success and take a moment to appreciate your resilience and determination.*

» **Self-Compassion Mantra:** *Develop a*

self-compassion mantra or affirmation that resonates with you. Repeat it to yourself regularly, especially during moments of self-doubt or criticism, to cultivate self-compassion and build resilience.

» **Gratitude Jar:** *Start a gratitude jar and write down moments of progress, achievements, or acts of self-compassion on small notes. Place them in the jar and revisit them whenever you need a reminder of your growth and self-care efforts.*

» **Self-Celebration Collage:** *Create a collage using images, quotes, and words that represent your achievements and moments of self-compassion. Display it in a prominent place as a visual reminder of your progress and self-worth.*

» **Positive Self-Talk Challenge:** *Challenge yourself to replace self-critical thoughts with self-compassionate and encouraging statements for a day. Pay attention to how this shift in self-talk impacts your mood and overall well-being.*

» **Progress Journal:** *Start a progress journal to track your personal growth journey. Write down milestones, lessons learned, and moments of self-compassion. Reflect on your entries regularly to appreciate your progress.*

- **Kindness to Others:** *Practice acts of kindness and compassion towards others. Engaging in altruistic behavior can reinforce the value of kindness and self-compassion, fostering a positive mindset and reinforcing your own growth.*

Quiz Answers for Section VI.B: Celebrating Progress and Practicing Self-Compassion

151. The main focus of Section VI.B is celebrating progress and practicing self-compassion for sustaining personal growth.

152. Celebrating progress is important because it reinforces positive behaviors, boosts motivation, and cultivates a sense of accomplishment. It also provides encouragement during challenging times.

153. **False.** Self-compassion involves treating yourself with kindness, understanding, and acceptance, especially in the face of mistakes or failures.

154. Celebrating progress and practicing self-compassion contribute to sustaining personal growth by fostering self-confidence, maintaining motivation, nurturing resilience, and improving overall well-being.

155. Examples may include sharing your achievements with a supportive friend or family member, treating yourself to a small reward, journaling about your progress, or engaging in a self-care activity you enjoy.

156. Practicing self-compassion during setbacks or failures helps you develop resilience, learn from mistakes, maintain a positive self-image, and bounce back more effectively.

157. **False.** Self-compassion is a sign of strength and self-care. It acknowledges that everyone

makes mistakes and experiences difficulties, and it promotes a nurturing attitude towards oneself.

158. Self-compassion helps you maintain motivation and resilience by offering support and understanding during challenging times. It prevents self-criticism from undermining your progress and encourages a positive mindset.

159. Gratitude plays a role in celebrating progress by helping you appreciate your achievements and the efforts that led to them. It also promotes self-compassion by shifting the focus from shortcomings to blessings and positive experiences.

160. You can integrate the practice of self-compassion into your daily life by being mindful of your self-talk, practicing self-forgiveness, engaging in self-care activities, and surrounding yourself with supportive and compassionate people.

Embracing a Lifelong Learning Mindset

In our quest for personal growth and self-mastery, it is vital to embrace a lifelong learning mindset. The journey of unleashing our inner potential is not a destination but an ongoing process of growth and discovery. By adopting a mindset that values continuous learning, we open ourselves up to new opportunities, expand our knowledge and skills, and cultivate the adaptability necessary for lasting success. In this section, we will explore the importance of embracing a lifelong learning mindset and provide practical strategies to foster a love for learning and personal development.

The Power of Lifelong Learning

Lifelong learning is a mindset that recognizes the value of seeking knowledge, acquiring new skills, and pursuing personal development throughout our lives. Here's why embracing a lifelong learning mindset is crucial:

» **Adaptability and Growth:** *In today's fast-paced and ever-evolving world, the ability to adapt and grow is essential. By embracing lifelong learning, we develop the agility and flexibility to navigate change and seize opportunities. We become comfortable with stepping out of our comfort zones and embracing new challenges, which leads to* *personal and professional growth.*

» **Expanding Knowledge and Skills:** *Lifelong learning allows us to expand our knowledge and acquire new skills. It opens doors to new ideas, perspectives, and areas of expertise. Whether it's through formal education, workshops, online courses, or self-study, every learning opportunity adds to our intellectual toolkit and enriches our understanding of the world.*

» **Building Confidence:** *The process of learning and acquiring new skills boosts our confidence. As we develop competence in different areas, we gain a sense of accomplishment and self-assurance. This confidence spills over into other aspects of our lives, empowering us to take on new challenges and pursue our goals with conviction.*

» **Cultivating Curiosity and Creativity:** *Lifelong learning nurtures our innate curiosity and creativity. It encourages us to ask questions, explore new ideas, and think critically. When we approach learning with an open and curious mind, we discover innovative solutions, unlock our creativity, and find inspiration in unexpected places.*

Strategies for Embracing Lifelong Learning

To embrace a lifelong learning mindset, consider incorporating the following strategies into your life:

- **Set Learning Goals:** *Define learning goals that align with your interests, passions, and areas of growth. These goals can be short-term or long-term, specific or broad. Write them down and revisit them regularly to stay focused and motivated.*

- **Create a Learning Routine:** *Dedicate regular time for learning in your schedule. Treat it as a priority and commit to consistent effort. Whether it's a few minutes each day or a dedicated block of time each week, make learning a habit.*

- **Diversify Learning Methods:** *Explore various learning methods to cater to different learning styles and preferences. Read books, listen to podcasts, watch educational videos, attend workshops or seminars, engage in online courses, join discussion groups, or find a mentor. Experiment with different approaches to find what resonates with you.*

- **Cultivate a Growth Mindset:** *Embrace a growth mindset, which is the belief that our abilities can be developed through dedication and hard work. Embrace challenges, view* *failures as opportunities for learning, and approach setbacks with resilience. Remember that progress is more important than perfection, and that mistakes are stepping stones to growth.*

» **Seek Feedback and Reflection:** *Actively seek feedback on your progress and areas for improvement. Reflect on your learning journey, celebrate your achievements, and identify areas where you can continue to grow. Regular self-reflection enhances self-awareness and facilitates continuous improvement.*

» **Embrace New Experiences:** *Step outside your comfort zone and embrace new experiences that broaden your horizons. Travel to new places, engage in different hobbies, volunteer for unfamiliar tasks, or explore diverse cultures. These experiences provide fresh perspectives and stimulate personal growth.*

» **Connect and Collaborate:** *Engage with a community of learners and like-minded individuals who share your passion for personal development. Join or create study groups, attend conferences or meetups, participate in online forums, or connect with individuals through social media.*

Collaborative learning encourages knowledge sharing, sparks discussions, and offers support and inspiration.

» **Apply and Teach:** *Actively apply what you learn to real-life situations. Practice the skills you acquire and find opportunities to teach others. Sharing your knowledge and expertise not only reinforces your own learning but also contributes to the growth of others.*

Remember, embracing a lifelong learning mindset is not about accumulating knowledge for the sake of it but about applying what you learn to enhance your personal and professional life. It's an ongoing process that requires curiosity, dedication, and an open mind. By cultivating a love for learning and seeking continuous improvement, you unlock your true potential and embark on a journey of self-mastery and lasting success.

In the concluding section, we will reflect on your transformative journey of unleashing your inner potential and offer guidance on how to embrace your transformed self in all areas of your life.

Quiz Questions for Section VI.C: Embracing a Lifelong Learning Mindset

161. What is the main focus of Section VI.C?
162. Why is embracing a lifelong learning mindset important for personal growth?
163. **True or False**: A fixed mindset is conducive to continuous learning and personal development.
164. What are some ways you can foster a lifelong learning mindset?
165. How does embracing a lifelong learning mindset contribute to sustaining personal growth?
166. **True or False**: Learning opportunities are only found in formal educational settings.
167. Name three strategies for expanding your knowledge and skills outside of traditional learning environments.
168. How can curiosity and a thirst for knowledge support your personal growth journey?
169. Discuss the relationship between a growth mindset and embracing a lifelong learning mindset.
170. How can you integrate the practice of lifelong learning into your daily life?

Exercises for Section VI.C: Embracing a Lifelong Learning Mindset

» **Learning Bucket List:** *Create a list of topics, skills, or subjects you have always wanted to learn more about. Set a goal to explore and learn about at least one of these items within a specific timeframe.*

» **TED Talk Challenge:** *Watch a TED Talk on a topic that piques your interest. Take notes and reflect on what you learned. Share the key takeaways with a friend or family member and engage in a discussion about the talk.*

» **Book Club Exploration:** *Join or start a book club focused on personal development and lifelong learning. Each month, select a book that expands your knowledge or challenges your perspectives. Engage in thoughtful discussions with fellow club members.*

» **Online Course Adventure:** *Enroll in an online course or MOOC (Massive Open Online Course) that aligns with your interests or professional development goals. Dedicate time each week to engage with the course materials, complete assignments, and connect with fellow learners.*

- **Mentorship Experience:** *Seek out a mentor who can guide you in a specific area of interest or expertise. Meet with your mentor regularly to learn from their experiences, seek advice, and gain valuable insights.*

- **Podcast Exploration:** *Find educational podcasts related to your interests or personal growth goals. Listen to episodes during your commute or downtime, and take notes on the key ideas or lessons you discover.*

- **Workshop or Seminar Attendance:** *Attend a workshop or seminar on a topic that intrigues you. Engage actively in discussions, ask questions, and network with other participants to broaden your perspectives and knowledge.*

- **Reflective Journaling:** *Dedicate time each day or week to journal about what you have learned, discovered, or explored. Reflect on the value and impact of continuous learning on your personal growth journey.*

- **Community Engagement:** *Get involved in your local community by joining clubs, organizations, or groups that focus on learning, skill development, or personal growth. Contribute your knowledge and expertise while learning from others.*

» **Expert Interviews:** *Reach out to experts in your field of interest or those who have achieved success in an area you aspire to. Conduct interviews or schedule meetings to learn from their experiences, gain insights, and apply their wisdom to your own journey.*

Quiz Answers for Section VI.C: Embracing a Lifelong Learning Mindset

161. The main focus of Section VI.C is embracing a lifelong learning mindset.
162. Embracing a lifelong learning mindset is important for personal growth because it promotes continuous growth, expands knowledge and skills, fosters adaptability, and encourages curiosity and exploration.
163. **False.** A fixed mindset, characterized by a belief that abilities are fixed and unchangeable, hinders continuous learning and personal development.
164. Some ways to foster a lifelong learning mindset include seeking new challenges, staying curious, being open to different perspectives, seeking feedback, and embracing a growth mindset.
165. Embracing a lifelong learning mindset contributes to sustaining personal growth by promoting adaptability, expanding knowledge and skills, fostering personal and professional development, and cultivating a growth-oriented mindset.
166. **False.** Learning opportunities can be found in various settings beyond formal education, such as online courses, workshops, books, podcasts, and interactions with mentors and experts.
167. Strategies for expanding knowledge and skills outside of traditional learning environments include reading books, attending workshops

or seminars, participating in online courses, engaging in self-directed learning, networking with experts, and exploring educational resources online.

168. Curiosity and a thirst for knowledge support personal growth by encouraging continuous learning, inspiring exploration and innovation, fostering a growth mindset, and expanding one's understanding of the world.

169. A growth mindset and embracing a lifelong learning mindset go hand in hand. Both involve believing in the potential for growth, seeking challenges, embracing failures as learning opportunities, and persisting in the face of obstacles.

170. You can integrate the practice of lifelong learning into your daily life by staying curious, seeking new experiences, reading books, engaging in reflective thinking, pursuing personal interests, connecting with mentors, and actively seeking opportunities for growth and development.

VII. Conclusion

Reflecting on Your Journey and Embracing Your Transformed Self

As you reach the conclusion of your transformative journey of unleashing your inner potential, it is essential to take the time for reflection and introspection. This final section serves as a guide to help you reflect on how far you have come, acknowledge the growth you have experienced, and embrace your transformed self with open arms. By looking back at the lessons learned and the progress made, you can reinforce the positive changes in your life and set a solid foundation for a future filled with continued growth and personal fulfillment.

The Power of Reflection

Reflection is a powerful tool that allows us to gain insight and understanding from our experiences. It provides an opportunity to step back, take stock of our journey, and make sense of the lessons learned along the way. By reflecting on your personal growth and mindset mastery, you can reinforce the positive changes you have made, identify areas for further improvement, and celebrate your accomplishments.

To engage in meaningful reflection, consider the following practices:

- » **Journaling:** *Set aside dedicated time to journal about your journey. Write about the challenges you faced, the breakthroughs you experienced, and the lessons you learned. Explore your emotions, thoughts, and insights, allowing yourself to delve deeper into your personal transformation.*

- » **Mindful Contemplation:** *Practice mindfulness and meditation to create a calm and focused state of mind. Use this time to reflect on your personal growth, recognizing the shifts in your mindset, and acknowledging the positive changes in your thoughts, emotions, and behaviors.*

- » **Guided Questions:** *Ask yourself thought-provoking questions that encourage introspection. Some examples include:*

How have my beliefs and self-perception evolved throughout this journey?

What were the most significant challenges I faced, and how did I overcome them?

What have I learned about myself, my strengths, and my areas for improvement?

How have my relationships and support systems evolved as a result of my personal growth?

How has my perspective on success, happiness, and fulfillment changed?

What are the key lessons I want to carry forward from this transformative experience?

Celebrating Your Accomplishments

As you reflect on your journey, it is crucial to celebrate your accomplishments, no matter how small or significant they may seem. Recognize the progress you have made, the obstacles you have overcome, and the personal milestones you have achieved. Celebrating your accomplishments reinforces positive reinforcement and builds confidence, motivating you to continue on your path of personal growth.

Consider the following ways to celebrate your accomplishments:

» **Acknowledge and Appreciate:** *Take the time to acknowledge and appreciate your achievements. Write them down, create a gratitude list, or share them with a trusted friend or mentor. This process helps you recognize your growth and builds a positive mindset.*

» **Reward Yourself:** *Treat yourself to a well-deserved reward or indulgence. It could be* *something as simple as enjoying your favorite meal, taking a day off to relax, or treating yourself to a meaningful gift. These rewards serve as reminders of your progress and the value you place on your personal growth.*

» **Share Your Success:** *Share your accomplishments with those who have supported you throughout your journey. Celebrate with your loved ones, friends, or mentors who have been there to cheer you on and offer guidance. Sharing your success not only strengthens your relationships but also reinforces your commitment to personal growth.*

Embracing Your Transformed Self

As you reflect on your journey and celebrate your accomplishments, it's time to embrace your transformed self fully. This is a pivotal moment where you acknowledge the positive changes you have made and commit to living a life aligned with your newfound mindset and potential.

To embrace your transformed self, consider the following steps:

» **Gratitude and Self-Appreciation:** *Express gratitude for the growth and transformation you have experienced. Appreciate yourself for the commitment, resilience, and effort you* *have invested in your personal development. Cultivate self-compassion and treat yourself with kindness and understanding.*

- » **Embody Your Values:** *Identify the values that have emerged or strengthened throughout your journey. These values serve as guiding principles for your actions and decisions. Embody them in your daily life, aligning your thoughts, words, and behaviors with your authentic self.*

- » **Set Intentional Goals:** *Build upon your personal growth by setting intentional goals that reflect your transformed self. Use the knowledge and insights gained during your journey to create meaningful objectives that align with your values, aspirations, and vision for the future. These goals will continue to drive your personal growth and contribute to your overall success and fulfillment.*

- » **Share Your Wisdom:** *Pay it forward by sharing your wisdom and insights with others. Become a mentor or guide for individuals who are starting their own journeys of personal growth. Your experiences and lessons learned can inspire and empower others on their path to unlocking their inner potential.*

As you embrace your transformed self, remember that personal growth is an ongoing process. Continue to nurture your mindset, prioritize self-care, and embrace the lifelong learning mindset you have cultivated. Stay open to new experiences, challenges, and opportunities for growth, knowing that you have the power within you to overcome obstacles and create a life of lasting success and fulfillment.

Conclusion

In conclusion, "Unleashing Your Inner Potential: The Power of Mindset Mastery" has taken you on a transformative journey of self-discovery and personal growth. From understanding the power of mindset to mastering your thoughts, emotions, and actions, you have gained valuable insights and practical tools for unleashing your true potential. By nurturing relationships, practicing self-care, and embracing a lifelong learning mindset, you have set a solid foundation for sustained personal growth.

Through reflection, celebration, and the embrace of your transformed self, you have integrated your newfound mindset and growth into all aspects of your life. You have the power to continue your journey of personal development, contributing to your success, happiness, and fulfillment.

As you move forward, remember that your mindset is a powerful tool. Harness its potential, believe in yourself, and persevere through challenges. Embrace the journey, for it is in the process of growth that you will discover the true power within you. May you continue to unleash your inner potential and create a life of purpose, meaning, and lasting success.

Quiz Questions for Section VII.A: Reflecting on Your Journey and Embracing Your Transformed Self

171. What is the main focus of Section VII.A?
172. Why is reflecting on your journey important for personal growth?
173. **True or False**: Reflecting on your journey only involves looking at your achievements and successes.
174. What are some ways you can practice reflection in your daily life?
175. How can reflecting on your journey help you embrace your transformed self?
176. **True or False**: Reflection is a one-time activity and does not require ongoing practice.
177. Name three benefits of incorporating reflection into your personal growth journey.
178. How can gratitude play a role in the process of reflection?
179. Discuss the relationship between self-awareness and reflection.
180. How can you apply the insights gained from reflection to future decision-making and personal development?

Exercises for Section VII.A: Reflecting on Your Journey and Embracing Your Transformed Self

» **Reflective Journaling:** *Set aside dedicated time each day or week to write in a journal. Reflect on your experiences, challenges, successes, and personal growth. Write down insights, lessons learned, and areas for further development.*

» **Guided Meditation:** *Engage in guided meditation sessions focused on reflection and self-discovery. Use prompts or visualizations to guide your thoughts and encourage deep introspection.*

» **Vision Board Creation:** *Create a vision board that represents your personal growth journey. Include images, quotes, and symbols that reflect your aspirations, achievements, and the person you want to become. Regularly review your vision board and reflect on your progress.*

» **Conversation Circles:** *Organize or join a conversation circle with like-minded individuals. Share your personal growth journey, challenges, and insights with others, and actively listen to their stories. Engage in meaningful discussions that encourage*

» **Letter to Your Past Self:** *Write a letter to your past self, offering guidance, encouragement, and insights based on what you have learned on your personal growth journey. Reflect on how far you have come and express gratitude for the lessons learned.*

» **Gratitude Practice:** *Develop a gratitude practice where you reflect on and express gratitude for the experiences, people, and lessons that have shaped your personal growth. Write a gratitude journal or share your gratitude with someone you appreciate.*

» **Retreat or Solo Getaway:** *Plan a retreat or solo getaway where you can disconnect from daily routines and dedicate time for introspection and reflection. Engage in activities such as journaling, hiking, meditation, or artistic expression to foster self-reflection.*

» **Timeline Exercise:** *Create a timeline of your personal growth journey, noting significant milestones, challenges, and moments of transformation. Reflect on how each experience has shaped you and consider the lessons learned along the way.*

» **Mind Map Exploration:** *Use a mind*

map to visually represent your personal growth journey. Start with a central concept representing your transformed self and branch out with various subtopics related to your growth, achievements, challenges, and aspirations.

» **Future Self Visualization:** *Engage in a visualization exercise where you imagine your future self, fully embracing your transformed state. Visualize the qualities, achievements, and fulfillment you desire, and reflect on the steps you need to take to align your present actions with that vision.*

Quiz Answers for Section VII.A: Reflecting on Your Journey and Embracing Your Transformed Self

171. The main focus of Section VII.A is reflecting on your journey and embracing your transformed self.
172. Reflecting on your journey is important for personal growth because it allows you to gain self-awareness, identify patterns, learn from experiences, and make informed decisions for future development.
173. **False.** Reflection involves examining both achievements and challenges, as well as the lessons learned from them.
174. You can practice reflection in your daily life through activities like journaling, meditation, self-assessment, mindfulness, and seeking feedback from others.
175. Reflecting on your journey helps you embrace your transformed self by recognizing the progress you've made, understanding the changes you've undergone, and appreciating the growth you've experienced.
176. **False.** Reflection is an ongoing practice that benefits from regular engagement and consistent effort.
177. Benefits of reflection include increased self-awareness, improved decision-making, identification of growth areas, enhanced learning, a deeper sense of purpose, and increased gratitude and self-compassion.

178. Gratitude can play a role in reflection by helping you appreciate the experiences and people who have contributed to your personal growth and by fostering a positive mindset.

179. Self-awareness and reflection are interconnected because reflection encourages self-awareness, and self-awareness provides the foundation for effective reflection.

180. Insights gained from reflection can be applied to future decision-making and personal development by helping you make more informed choices, set meaningful goals, and adjust your strategies based on past experiences and lessons learned.

Keywords:

mindset mastery, inner potential, personal growth, unlocking true potential, lasting success, mind-body connection, limiting beliefs, self-sabotaging patterns, growth mindset, embracing challenges, visualization techniques, affirmations for success, taming the inner critic, overcoming negative self-talk, emotional intelligence, navigating emotions, harnessing positivity, building resilience, bouncing back from setbacks, purposeful goal setting, action plan creation, overcoming procrastination, creating healthy habits, cultivating empathy, effective communication skills, building healthy boundaries, support systems, role of mentorship, accountability practices, self-care strategies, mindfulness practices, celebrating progress, practicing self-compassion, lifelong learning mindset, reflecting on the journey, embracing transformation, power of mindset, self-improvement techniques, overcoming obstacles, positive mindset, personal development, achieving goals, empowerment strategies, self-discovery, overcoming challenges, emotional well-being, motivation techniques, goal achievement, self-confidence building, transformational journey

Full Summary:

"Unleashing Your Inner Potential: The Power of Mindset Mastery" is a groundbreaking guide that will empower you to unlock your true potential and achieve lasting success. This transformative book dives deep into the mind-body connection, helping you understand the immense power of your mindset in shaping your personal growth. With insights on identifying and overcoming limiting beliefs and self-sabotaging patterns, you'll cultivate a growth mindset, fearlessly embracing challenges and failures along the way. Through the art of visualization and affirmations, you'll manifest your desires and pave the path to extraordinary achievements.

Mastering your thoughts and emotions is a crucial step in this journey, and this book provides invaluable techniques to tame your inner critic and overcome negative self-talk. Discover the art of emotional intelligence, learning to navigate and harness your emotions for personal and professional success. Harness the power of gratitude and positivity as you cultivate a mindset that attracts abundance and joy into your life.

Building resilience is vital for bouncing back from setbacks, and this book equips you with the tools to develop unwavering resilience. Set purposeful goals, create action plans, and conquer procrastination as you establish healthy habits that support your growth.

Nurturing relationships and fostering support systems become cornerstones of your journey, enabling you to cultivate empathy, effective communication, and build healthy boundaries.

Sustaining personal growth is essential, and this book reveals the significance of self-care and mindfulness practices. Celebrate your progress and practice self-compassion as you embrace a lifelong learning mindset that fuels continuous development. Reflect on your journey, embrace your transformed self, and embark on a future brimming with possibilities.

With "Unleashing Your Inner Potential: The Power of Mindset Mastery," you'll embark on a transformative adventure of self-discovery, overcoming obstacles, and achieving your goals. Embrace the power of your mindset, tap into your inner potential, and create a life of lasting success and fulfillment. Begin your personal growth journey today and witness the incredible transformation that awaits you.

Short Summary:

Unleashing Your Inner Potential: The Power of Mindset Mastery is a transformative guide that empowers you to unlock your true potential and achieve lasting success.

With a focus on mindset mastery, this book reveals the untapped power of your mind and teaches you how to harness it to overcome obstacles and achieve remarkable growth.

From understanding the mind-body connection to cultivating a growth mindset, embracing challenges, and utilizing the art of visualization and affirmations, you'll learn to break free from limiting beliefs and self-sabotaging patterns.

Navigate your thoughts and emotions with emotional intelligence, gratitude, and positivity.

Build resilience, set purposeful goals, and overcome procrastination to take meaningful action.

Nurturing relationships, empathy, effective communication, healthy boundaries, and mentorship play crucial roles in your personal growth journey.

Sustain your progress through self-care, mindfulness practices, self-compassion, and a lifelong learning mindset.

Reflect on your journey, embrace your transformed self, and witness the remarkable results.

This book is a comprehensive roadmap to unleash your inner potential and live a life of fulfillment, abundance, and happiness.

Discover the power of mindset mastery today and embark on a transformative journey towards achieving your wildest dreams.

www.ingramcontent.com/pod-product-compliance
Lightning Source LLC
Chambersburg PA
CBHW070838160426
43192CB00012B/2230